HIGH DESERT YARDS AND GARDENS

High Desert
Yards and Gardens

Lynn Ellen Doxon

UNIVERSITY OF NEW MEXICO PRESS

ALBUQUERQUE

Library of Congress
Cataloging-in-Publication Data
Doxon, Lynn Ellen, 1951–
Hight desert yards and gardens/
Lynn Ellen Doxon.—1st ed.
p. cm.
Based on the author's Yard and garden
column published in the Albuquerque journal.
Includes index.
ISBN 0-8263-1909-2 (cloth).
ISBN 0-8263-1910-6 (pbk.)
1. Gardening—Southwest, New.
2. Desert gardening—Southwest, New.
1. Title.
SB453.2.S66D69 1999
635.9'525'09791—dc21 98-47385
CIP
Designed by
Sue Niewiarowski

CONTENTS

ACKNOWLEDGMENTS

I thank my husband, Robert Habiger,
and my mother, Lydia Doxon, for providing
the illustrations for this book and for
encouraging me throughout the process.
My deepest gratitude goes to Barbara Guth for
sticking with the book through difficult times
and providing help and encouragement
through the many revisions of the manuscript.
I also thank the many people who have faithfully
read and sent questions to the Yard and Garden Column
in the *Albuquerque Journal*, which provided
the material for this book.

INTRODUCTION

Gardening in the Southwest is notoriously difficult because of the soil and climate. At the same time it is ultimately rewarding because of the variety of plants that can be grown and the dramatic effect of a well-planned landscape. A strategically placed shade tree can make the difference between pleasant and unbearable in summertime. Shrubs and trees can stop the wind in winter and spring and prevent soil erosion. A small green area can have an amazing cooling effect on hot summer days. Even though water is becoming harder to get and more expensive, plants are essential to a pleasant living environment.

This book had its start in the Yard and Garden Column published in the *Albuquerque Journal*. That column, which I have written since 1988, provided much of the material in this book and has given me an understanding of the kinds of information southwestern gardeners need. In my column I try to combine scientific knowledge, experience, and common sense. These are the same elements I have tried to bring to this book.

Although I do not often get questions from readers about soil, it is the underlying cause of many problems for southwestern gardeners. Soil acts as a reservoir for the water and nutrients that plants need; it also provides a medium for the structural support of the plant. Some southwestern soils lack the ability to effectively perform either of these tasks. Soil improvement is a relatively simple process but it is never-ending and often requires heavy work. The effect of ongoing efforts to improve the soil are dramatic.

Great value is placed on a full-grown shade tree in this region of desert sun and expanding cities. Over the years readers have asked many questions about trees—how to select, care for, prune, and control pests and diseases on them—and these topics are covered in some detail. The table on pages 52–59 offers information about selection and use of trees.

Lawn care, another issue of concern to southwesterners, has become controversial in recent years because of water usage. The single most effective way to reduce water use in the Southwest is correct watering. Lawns often get two to three times the water they actually need. This causes disease and thatch problems.

Many gardening books have been produced for the Southwest in the past several years, but almost all of them focus on the conditions of the low desert in Arizona and California. Those that deal with high desert conditions are more suitable to the higher elevation areas of the same states. This book is based on conditions in New Mexico. Gardening conditions in New Mexico are not uniform. The range of climate zones is as great as that in the central part of the country from Michigan to Mississippi. Rainfall varies from quite arid through semiarid to temperate. Vegetation zones include three desert types, two grassland types, five forest zones, and the Great Basin. Before you begin gardening, you should determine the climate zone, rainfall, and native vegetation type of your area. Five different vegetation zones come together in Albuquerque and there is a 50 percent variation between the areas with the lowest average rainfall and the highest average rainfall in the city. Maps are included to help determine these factors on a general basis. Individual locations can be affected by microclimate factors that are too localized to be shown on a map.

Gardening in the Southwest is both challenging and rewarding. This book offers suggestions and advice for avid gardeners, casual gardeners, and beginning gardeners. Most U.S. garden books are written either for the eastern half of the United States or for the coastal and desert areas of the West, where freezing temperatures and winter storms are not a consideration. *The Southwestern Yard and Garden* provides information on gardening in the high desert and southern Rocky Mountains. Although it is written with New Mexico, specifically Albuquerque, in mind it will also be useful in parts of Colorado, Arizona, Utah, Nevada, Texas, and California.

CHAPTER I

Soil and Fertilizers

Southwestern soil is difficult soil. In most areas it has high pH, very low organic matter, and low nitrogen. It is often shallow and frequently gravely or rocky. In some parts of the Southwest what passes for soil is rocks or gravel.

Soil is classified by texture: clay, silt, or sand. Loam is a soil of mixed texture. The first step in determining soil texture is to rub it between the thumb and fingers or in the palm of the hand. Sand particles will have a gritty feeling when they are dry. A moist ball of sand will fall apart easily. Silt has a talcum-like feel when it is dry and will stick together when squeezed but cannot be molded without falling apart. Clay has a harsh feeling when dry and is very sticky when wet. It will hold its shape when squeezed and can be molded into other shapes.

Most soils fall into the loam category, with a mixture of sand, silt, and clay. To determine how much clay, silt, and sand is in a loam soil, put a cup of the soil in a glass jar and fill the jar with water. Shake the mixture thoroughly and let it settle until the water is clear. Soil particles of different textures will settle at different rates, with sand on the bottom, silt next, and finally clay. Loam soils are the easiest to deal with. Sandy soil is easy to work but has little fertility or water-holding capacity. Clay will form hard clods if worked while it is wet and will be quite difficult to dig. Caliche and tuff, which are soft rock, and adobe soil, which is hard clay, are impossible to dig with a shovel when dry. In areas with adobe, caliche, or tuff, raised beds with "manufactured" soil made of top-soil from another area and plenty of compost should be constructed.

SOIL TESTING

A soil test will provide information on how to treat a particular soil. Along with the soil test results, you will receive recommendations on how much of what nutrients to apply. Microbial and chemical activity increases when the temperatures are warmer; as a result, more nutrients are released in the soil. A sample taken during warm weather will be a more accurate measure of the nutrients available to your plants. If the soil sample is taken in winter the results for nitrogen availability will be quite inaccurate, although nitrogen levels vary from day to day in any soil.

To take a soil sample, mark several sites that seem typical of the soil in the yard. At each site remove surface litter such as leaves, dry grass, or mulch. Dig a hole about six inches deep. With the shovel take a slice of soil one-half inch thick and six inches deep. Keep the slice on the shovel and cut a strip from the center with a knife. Put this center strip in a bucket and go on to the next site. Mix the soil from all the sites. Break up any clods or lumps and let the sample dry at room temperature. Do not use heat for drying. Put the sample in a paper bag inside a box and send it off to be tested. The more information you can provide about the soil, the better the results will be. Most soil-testing labs have information sheets, as well as boxes for mailing the samples.

Albuquerque residents can take their soil samples to the Albuquerque Garden Club Center on Lomas to have them tested by master gardeners. The center charges for the service but provides a detailed report, which is prepared with the home gardener in mind. Soil testing is also available from the Soil and Water Testing Lab at New Mexico State University. For most New Mexico residents this is the most convenient and least expensive way to get soil tested. Contact your county agent for a fee schedule and infor-mation on how to send your sam-ples to this lab. These tests are a-vailable to anyone in the state. A number of private soil-testing labs in the country will test your soil for varying fees. Home soil-test kits are accurate if the reagents are fresh and the tests are done prop-erly. Results from different labs will vary slightly depending on the microbial and chemical activ-ity of the sample, test methods used by that lab, and the techni-cian doing the tests. Do not be concerned if two samples from the same general area come back with slightly different results.

The basic tests that should be done are a test for pH, percent of soluble salts, percent of exchange-able sodium, percent of organic matter, texture, available phos-

---

Taking A Soil Sample

Mark several sites that seem typical of the soil in the yard.

Remove surface litter such as leaves, dry grass or mulch.

Dig a hole about six inches deep.

With the shovel take a slice of soil one half inch thick and six inches deep. Keep the slice on the shovel and cut a strip from the center with a knife.

Put this center strip in a bucket and go on to the next site. Mix the soil from all the sites.

Break any clods or lumps and let the sample dry at room temperature. Do not use heat for drying.

Put the sample in a paper bag inside a box and send it off to be tested.

---

phorous, and available potassium. Generally one or more tests of nitro-gen availability will also be conducted. These results should be used only as a general guide because nitrogen levels vary so.

pH

pH measures the level of alkalinity or acidity of the soil. Soil pH gener-ally ranges from 4.0 in acidic soils to 10.0 for the most alkaline soils. Soils with a pH of 8.5 or higher are very alkaline. Most plants grow best in soils that are neutral to slightly acid. A number of compounds can cause high pH, but in the Southwest an alkaline soil is generally one that is high in calcium. It may also have a variety of magnesium salts in it and may even have quite a bit of sodium.

A white crust is one indicator that soil is alkaline. In chemical terms, alkaline means more negative hydroxide ions than positive hydrogen ions are present in the soil. Alkaline soils tend to tie up some nutrients that plants need, such as iron and zinc. To make soil less alkaline, add organic matter and sulfur. The sulfur will form sulfuric acid if there is enough activity by microscopic organisms. The organic matter helps promote the microbial activity. Even organic matter by itself can help through the formation of humic acid. Commercial additives are available to make a soil more acid. Be sure to use a product that has been formulated as a soil additive. Do not try to combat alkalinity by adding battery acid or other strong acid to the soil.

Most New Mexico soils never require lime. Lime is applied to neutralize acid soils. A few isolated locations in New Mexico have acid soil, but most often the soil is already too alkaline.

SALTY SOIL

Chemically many compounds are salts. The common meaning of salty soils, however, is a high-sodium soil. A soil that is a slick clay when it is wet, takes a long time to dry out, and cracks when it does dry out, may be a high-sodium soil. Only a soil test can determine how salty a soil is. Total soluble salts above .30 percent can be a problem.

The simplest way to correct salt problems in light soils is to leach the salts below the root zone. If the salinity hazard is high and the irrigation water also contains large amounts of sodium, add 40 percent more water than the plants need in order to leach salt below the root zone. See specific instructions on irrigation (chapter 3) to determine how much water plants in different soils would normally need.

Heavy soils high in sodium usually have low permeability and poor structure. The soil does not drain well. To relieve the problem, add gypsum to replace the sodium with calcium, then leach the soil to wash the sodium away. A pH value above 8.0 indicates a high level of calcium in the soil. Add sulfur and organic matter to reduce the effects of the calcium.

Very alkaline or very salty soil makes gardening difficult. Both can be compounded by poor drainage. A crust on the surface of the soil may be an indication of poor drainage. Install drain tiles and leach the soil before planting. Drainage might also be improved by mixing large quantities of organic material into the top twenty-four inches of the soil. This is more work than installing drain tiles but is less expensive if you have a free source of organic material. Mix the organic material well with the existing soil so there is no layering effect. Layers will make drainage worse.

ORGANIC MATTER

Organic material such as animal manure or compost has other advantages when added to the soil. The percentage of organic matter, which is related to the amount of nitrogen in the soil, affects the ability of soil to hold water and nutrients. The ideal amount of organic matter is 3 percent, although southwestern soils almost never have that high a percentage. Mix organic matter into the soil whenever possible. Sawdust or wood chips are effective when mixed with manure or nitrogen fertilizer but should not be used alone.

Chicken manure is one of the best organic fertilizers. It is high in nitrogen if it has not been stored in the open for extended periods. It has fewer weed seeds than horse manure unless weedy bedding material is mixed with it. It is lower in salt than steer manure. Fresh chicken manure has too much nitrogen in it to be applied in the root zone of actively growing plants. Excess nitrogen will prevent the plant from absorbing enough water, thus causing the tips of the leaves to dry out and look as if they have been burned. Fresh manure that has been mixed with bedding material like straw, ground corncobs, sawdust, or other dry plant material will increase nutrient levels and the amount of organic material in the soil. Mixing the manure with other material also helps reduce odors. Dig the mixture into vegetable gardens and annual flower beds or use it as a mulch around trees, shrubs, and perennials. Fresh manure may be put on the soil at least a month before planting or put in a pile to age properly.

Aged manure has few water soluble nutrients, but it increases the organic matter in the soil. Late fall is a good time to do this. In vegetable gardens and annual beds, till the manure in before the ground freezes. In perennial beds the manure can be used as a mulch. Earthworms and other soil organisms will mix it into the soil over time. A thin dressing of aged manure can also be used as a topdressing on lawns. As the manure breaks down it will help break down thatch.

Many commercial products are not useful. Humates are decomposed organic matter, about halfway between compost and coal. They are mined from areas similar to those with coal deposits. They contain minute amounts of nitrogen and some acid. But because they are in a form generally unavailable to plants, they do not act as effective soil conditioners. They may have micronutrients that will improve plant growth if the soil is deficient in that micronutrient.

COMPOST

Compost is a good source of humus, as well as a good way to get rid of many waste plant materials from the yard and garden. Anything that was once alive can be composted. Yard wastes, such as fallen leaves, grass clippings, weeds (without seeds), and the remains of garden plants, make excellent compost. Woody yard wastes can be chipped or shredded and added to the compost or used as mulch.

Care must be taken when composting kitchen scraps. Meat, bones, and fatty foods such as salad dressings, cheese, or leftover cooking oil should not be used in the compost pile as they attract rodents and other animals. Kitchen scraps should be buried in the center of the compost pile to avoid attracting insects.

The compost pile is a teaming microbial farm. Bacteria start the process of decaying organic matter. They are the first to break down plant tissue and the most numerous and effective composters. Fungi and protozoans soon join the bacteria. Somewhat later in the cycle, centipedes, millipedes, beetles, and earthworms do their part.

Everything organic has a ratio of carbon to nitrogen (C/N) in its tissues ranging from 500:1 for sawdust to 15:1 for table scraps. A C/N ratio of 30:1 is ideal for the activity of compost microbes. This balance can be achieved by mixing two parts grass clippings (20:1) with one part fallen leaves (60:1). Other materials such as garden wastes can be used. Materials can be layered to arrive at the proper proportions but should then be completely mixed to facilitate the composting process. Although the C/N ratio of 30:1 is ideal for fast, hot compost, which most effectively kills weed seeds and disease organisms, a higher ratio will be adequate for a slower compost. A compost pile with a ratio of 50:1 may take as long as two years to be ready for use.

Coffee grounds and tea leaves are excellent organic soil supplements, especially on our alkaline soils. The dried grounds are about 2 percent nitrogen, with small amounts of phosphorous and potassium. They are also a favorite of earthworms, which can further improve the soil. The white mold that grows on them is a fungus that helps break down decaying organic matter but will not invade healthy plants. Coffee grounds and tea leaves may be used directly on the ground or in the compost pile.

On the other hand, wood ashes are extremely alkaline and can cause all sorts of problems in our soil. They also have a high potassium content, and most southwestern soils do not need a lot of potassium. Dispose of wood ashes in the trash rather than the compost bin.

Most weed seeds should not be put in the compost pile. Properly heating compost will kill some weed seeds but not hard-coated seeds like goat-heads or bindweed. Many weed seeds will continue to ripen on the plant even after the plant is pulled. If a green plant with developing seeds is put into the compost pile, the seeds may still ripen in the pile. Some weeds are a bigger problem than others. Weeds that would be fairly easy to pull if they come up again next year might be put in the compost pile, but if seeds have formed, weeds should be disposed of in the trash.

The more surface area the microorganisms have to work on, the faster the materials decompose. Chopping garden wastes with a shovel or machete or running them through a shredding machine or lawn mower will speed composting. Both water and air are required by the compost-ing organisms. The pile should be moist but not soggy. The materials should be about as damp as a wrung out sponge.

A properly decomposing compost pile has a warm center and does not have a disagreeable odor. If the center of the pile is cool, add more high-nitrogen materials such as grass clippings or appropriate kitchen wastes. An odor of ammonia coming from the pile indicates it is either too wet or has too much nitrogen. Mix in some dry, low-nitrogen material like sawdust, leaves, or even shredded newspaper. Turn the pile every few weeks for faster, more complete decomposition.

Compost can be placed in bins constructed of wood and screening mate-rial, placed in a pile directly on the soil, or composted in a pit in the soil. Compost bins can be simple or complex. Three bins are convenient: one in which to build a new pile as materials become available, one in which composting is actively taking place, and one that holds finished compost.

LEAF MOLD

Two of the biggest sources of garbage in the city, grass clippings and leaves, are really not garbage. They are valuable fertilizer and organic matter. If a lawn is properly cared for, grass clippings do not have to be picked up.

If only a few small leaves are on the lawn, like the leaves of honeylocust trees, they can be chopped with a lawn mower and left on the lawn. If there are enough leaves to cover the grass, they should be removed so they do not smother the grass. Use them to make leaf mold. Leaf mold, the broken down remains of leaves, is the rich, musty substance found on the floor of hardwood forests. To make leaf mold, rake the leaves and enclose them in some way, for example, a circle of chicken wire or a snow fence. The larger the pieces of leaf, the longer it will take them to break down. Chopping or shredding will speed the process. The work is done by microorganisms, which are already present in large numbers. They will increase rapidly if given the correct environment in which to do their work. Sprinkle the leaf pile anytime it is dry. Don't make it soggy at the bottom, but keep it damp. By spring the leaves will be broken down, the pile much smaller than the original. Leaf mold can be used as mulch in flower beds, under shrubs and trees, or in the vegetable garden. You will not have to purchase peat moss or other soil amendments, and the country's massive landfill problems will be reduced.

Because the microorganisms that break down the leaves produce some acidifying substances, leaf mold can create a slight improvement in extremely high soil pH. The improvement will not be significant, however, because tree leaves tend to have a pH level similar to the soil in which they are grown.

CHEMICAL FERTILIZERS

Southwestern soils are frequently very low in nitrogen, and it is often difficult to add enough nitrogen in organic forms in a single year. The nitrogen forms in chemical fertilizers are as available or more available to plants than organic forms of nitrogen. Nitrogen fertilizer should be applied according to the directions provided with a soil test or the recommendations in this book for the type of plant to be fertilized.

Heavy irrigation where excess nitrogen has been applied to the soil has resulted in the leaching of nitrates, a form of nitrogen, into rivers, streams, and underground aquifers. High levels of nitrates can cause death in small babies and young animals. City water supplies are regularly tested for nitrates. Private wells should also be tested on a regular basis.

Excess fertilization is an even bigger problem in urban areas than in farming areas. Accidentally applying too much fertilizer to a lawn will not immediately contaminate the water supply of the city. Grass roots are excellent filters and hold onto most of the fertilizer that is applied to lawn areas. But many urban residents regularly apply two to five times the necessary amount of fertilizer to their yards. This can result in large amounts of nitrates being washed into the river or groundwater supplies downstream. Not only is the water contaminated but the plants are not getting the fertilizer, so the cost and effort of applying it has been wasted.

Overfertilization can be avoided three ways. One is to use no manufactured sources of fertilizer, using instead limited amounts of manure or compost. Many people are not satisfied with this because of the difficulty of spreading the material and the high salt content of many manures.

Another way is to apply chemical fertilizers in several small doses throughout the growing season. Read the directions on the package of fertilizer. For example, if it recommends one cup of fertilizer for one hundred square feet, apply one-fourth cup per month from April through July. This is especially important on sandy soils. Lawns can be fertilized until about a month before the time they normally become dormant for the winter. See specific schedules under lawns in chapter 4. Do not fertilize trees after July 4.

A third way is to use controlled-release fertilizers according to the directions on the package. Controlled-release fertilizers allow only a small amount of fertilizer into the soil at a time, preventing overfertilization. They can be applied less frequently than other chemical fertilizers. They are, however, more expensive than some other types of fertilizers.

SUPPLEMENTS

In recent years several products have come out that promise to increase the water-holding capacity of soils. Gels made from complex starches seem to live up to the claims made for them. But research shows that while gels called polyacrylamide hydrophilic gels did indeed increase the water-holding capacity of the soil when the soil was watered using deionized water, the effect almost disappeared when the water contained significant amounts of calcium or magnesium ions. Some water in the Southwest contains enough ions to reduce the effectiveness of the gels by 50 percent in one watering and repeated watering may reduce the effect to almost nothing. In addition, the ions in the soil could dissolve in the water and be deposited in the gels. Therefore do not use polyacrylamide hydrophilic gels in southwestern soil.

PREPARATION

Starting a yard around a new home can be difficult. To increase your chances of success, pick up any debris or cement chunks left behind by construction workers. Then till in as much organic matter as possible, grass clippings, leaves, manure, compost. Up to four inches of manure on the entire yard would not be too much for this first treatment. Add a little ammonium sulfate to make sure the microorganisms have enough nitrogen to break down all the organic matter you have tilled in, then plant a cover crop such as clover or annual ryegrass. Clover fixes nitrogen, but it is difficult to eradicate once it is established. Spread the seed for the cover crop on the ground, cover with a very light mulch, and sprinkle it to get it to sprout. Many of the weed seeds in the soil or the organic matter you added will also sprout. For now, think of them as additional green manure. When the green manure crop is well established but before anything goes to seed, till it all under. If the weather turns cold early, the crop may be frozen before it is tilled in. If this happens, prepare a small area for early spring vegetables if desired and leave the rest untilled. In the spring, begin watering again. Another green manure crop will come up. As each area is prepared for planting, till the cover crop under. After planting, put a heavy organic mulch on the ground to continue conditioning the soil and suppress the weeds. Once the weather warms up in the spring, have a soil test done. Wait until the soil has warmed up to at least 50°F so the microorganisms in the soil will have had a chance to make some of the nutrients in the organic matter available to plants. Use this soil test to determine how much fertilizer to add.

Prepare the entire yard in this way, then begin planning for specific landscape uses by installing sprinklers and sod, drip systems, and various other landscape features. Taking the extra time to prepare the yard will result in much more satisfactory results from all your landscape plantings.

MULCHING

One of the secrets to getting plants to survive in sandy soil is to mulch them heavily. Mulch also helps prevent crusting of clay soil. It keeps the soil cool and helps retain water. Plant seeds or bedding plants. When they are established, put at least three inches of organic mulch over the beds.

Save leaves in a wire enclosure to use as mulch next year. If there is not enough mulch available, haul in old spoiled hay, leaves from other people's yards, bark chips, or well-aged manure. In vegetable beds or annual flower beds, till or dig the mulch into the soil in the fall and bring in new mulch in the spring. Over several years rich soil can be built out of sand or clay.

Many materials can be used as mulch, including rocks, gravel, manure, compost, leaves, and sawdust. Sawdust used alone as a mulch tends to pack down and form a crust, but it can be spread on the soil, sprinkled with an inexpensive nitrogen fertilizer or a layer of manure, and mixed thoroughly with the first several inches of soil. Sawdust makes a great soil conditioner, improving the texture of clay and increasing the water-holding capacity of sandy soils, but as it decomposes nitrogen will be tied up, so you must add extra nitrogen.

STERILANTS

In an effort to control weeds, many people use soil sterilants. Unfortunately, if a true soil sterilant has been applied there is not much that can be done by subsequent residents. Soil sterilants will kill trees if their roots penetrate the treated area. Soil treated with a soil sterilant cannot be used to grow anything for several years. In a yard that has been treated with sterilants, keep the soil covered with rock, bark chips, or some other heavy mulch to keep it from eroding. Do not use plastic under the mulch. Buy several large tubs or build planters and set them around the yard. Fill them with topsoil from another location, then plant flowers, shrubs, and small trees in the tubs. When weeds start appearing through the mulch, try planting a few annual flowers in the soil. If they survive, proceed with landscape plans.

CHAPTER 2

Landscaping

The difference in property value between an attractively landscaped lot and a yard covered with lava rock or weeds can be 15 percent or more. One reason is that rocks can increase air-conditioning costs by up to 20 percent, depending on the location and microclimate. Plants also have soothing psychological effects, and most people will feel more comfortable in a house surrounded by green plants than by red or black rock. Rocks are generally used because people want a low-maintenance landscape, but using a few carefully selected native plants will increase property values. The yard need not take constant care and watering, but it should be green and inviting, without being overgrown or unkempt.

PLANNING

An attractive and useful landscape starts with a careful plan. To determine how each section of the yard should be used, create what landscape architects call a program. Where should the service area be placed for easy access to garbage cans or a storage shed? How will it be screened from the rest of the yard? Is a play area that is easily visible from the kitchen or living room needed for small children? How much space is needed for entertainment? A dog run? Off-street parking for extra vehicles? First, list things a landscape can provide down the left side of a sheet of paper. The list can include such things as privacy, recreation, food production, fuel conservation, color, wind protection, parking, pet areas, wildlife, storage, compost pile, barbecue area. Also list attributes of the environment that are important. These may include such things as ease of maintenance, a quiet, woodsy atmosphere, or open space. Next to each of these, list the requirements of that element. For example, a vegetable garden needs good soil, relatively flat land, sun, and protec‑ tion from wildlife. On the right side of the paper make three columns. Label them high, medium, and low. In these columns check how impor‑ tant each attribute is to you. Then list the elements of high importance in order of priority.

Make a scale drawing of the lot with all the permanent features shown in ink. If a patio or other major feature will be added in a few years, put that in the plan in pencil. Place tracing paper over the drawing and use it to make a diagram of the relationship of landscape elements. Decide where shade trees or vines are needed and where bright-colored flowers would look best. Are there slopes that need to be retained? Poor views that need to be hidden or beautiful views that need to be left open? See if areas are available that meet the requirements for the elements that are important. If the entire yard is steep and sloping, either eliminate the vegetable garden, or terrace a part of the yard, depending on the impor‑ tance of the vegetable garden. If open space is more important than color, you may want to eliminate annual flower beds. Place items so they are in the best relationship with each other. For example, the compost pile should be near the garden; the storage area for the lawn mower near the lawn. Draw circles or bubbles to represent each area. When the place‑ ment of all the areas is satisfactory, put another piece of tracing paper over the base plan and draw them in more accurately. At that point start determining the type of plants that fit the plan. Don't write in specific plants yet, just determine whether the plant should be a small tree, a rounded shrub, an upright shrub, a grouping of annual or perennial flowers, or a ground cover. Consider color and interest in all seasons.

Caring for the yard will be easier if grass is planned only where it has a purpose, such as entertaining or children's play area. Front lawns are seldom used, and if you do not like to mow grass, consider other plantings in the front. Plant shrubs and perennials that are easy to care for in this climate. If an attractive native shrub or yucca appears voluntarily in the yard, leave it or transplant it to a more appropriate location.

Draw in the mature size of the trees, shrubs, and perennials on the plan. Make sure the entrance to the house will remain visible and

---

Using Plants for Home Security

Avoid large, dense plantings in front of the door

Place low shrubs below windows

Landscape with heavy groundcovers or tall plants around graffiti targets

Cover walls with vines

Block potential access sites with thorny shrubs

---

accessible so visitors don't have to fight their way through a juniper jungle to get to the front door. Don't plant too close to a sidewalk in front of or alongside the lot. Be especially careful of this when planting thorny shrubs or evergreens. Try to balance the plantings so not all the large plants are on one side of the yard. Plan for a variety of plants. In that way if conditions are poor for some plants or a disease outbreak kills them, the landscape will not be devastated.

Two of the biggest landscaping problems are overplanting and planting trees that grow quickly and become too large for the space. Avoiding these problems can make installation of the landscape less expensive. Fast-growing trees, as a general rule, are weaker and shorter lived. They are also easier to propagate and cheaper, which accounts for their overuse. The average urban or suburban lot should not have more than one large tree on it; in soil where growing trees is particularly difficult, choose two or three medium or small trees. Place them carefully so they provide shade where it is needed. A medium-size tree on the southwest side of the house can significantly reduce cooling bills. If there is not enough space for a tree, a trellis with vines growing on it can serve the same purpose.

Once the plants are drawn in on the plan, with circles showing the mature size of the plant, visit several nurseries. Many nurseries have experienced and educated staff who can give free advice on the landscape plan and suggest plants. Check out prices in more than one place, and ask about warranties and free services that might be provided by the nurseries. If the plan includes some slow-growing trees, buy small ones but not the smallest available. Trees in five-gallon containers have a greater survival rate under adverse conditions than trees in one-gallon containers and a much greater survival rate than seedlings. However, they can get established and begin growing more quickly than large trees and in three to five years may have outgrown a tree that was larger at planting.

The same holds true for shrubs and perennials. "Special offers" in which several tiny perennial plants are held together with a rubber band and packed into a plastic bag are not a good buy no matter how low the price if none of the plants survive. On the other hand, an immature plant is a better buy than one that is full-size and ready to bloom; the smaller plant will establish its roots more quickly and have a better chance of surviving over the long run. If getting all the plants at once is too expensive, get the slowest-growing trees first and plan to buy more plants the next year.

After the new trees and shrubs are planted, the yard will look somewhat bare. Fill in with annuals. They will provide color and make the landscape look more finished but are inexpensive and won't crowd anything out next year. As the landscape matures, the perennial plants won't have to be removed and fewer annuals each year will be needed to serve as fillers. The character of the landscape will change over time, but with adequate planning the yard can be attractive right from the start.

XERISCAPE

Xeriscape is a word coined for landscape principles that have been known in the Southwest for centuries but have not been used effectively in our cities until recently. It basically means dry or limited-water-use landscaping. Landscaping accounts for as much as half the water used in non-industrial cities, and Xeriscape landscaping can cut landscape water use by 20 to 40 percent.

Seven principles should be followed in a Xeriscape.

1   Planning and design. Plan a Xeriscape the same way as any other landscape. Make a drawing of the property showing the buildings, utilities, and any other objects or plants that will be kept. Next analyze the yard and its needs as described above. Pay special attention to microclimates. What areas would make good oasis zones where those things that use a lot of water can be planted? What areas have the brightest sun and the most wind? These will be the driest areas. One planning stage is unique to Xeriscape planning. Mark whether specific groups of plants are to be very low water use, that is, never need to be watered, and which will be low-, medium-, or high-water-use. A few high-water-use plants are fine in a landscape if they are placed where they receive runoff from the roof or paved areas or are near a water source so they can be adequately irrigated.

Rocks and gravel can be used very effectively in a Xeriscape landscape to create certain effects, or even as a mulch. Remember, however, that covering too much of the yard with rocks can increase air-conditioning bills. Solid plastic should never be used under a rock mulch if plants are to be used in the yard. It prevents water and oxygen from penetrating the soil and limits the root area of plants. This leads to unhealthy plants. Use woven weed barrier or weed barrier cloth instead of plastic.

2   Using turf areas only where appropriate. Turf is the only suitable playing surface for many games, makes an excellent place for small children to play without getting dirty, and is a nice extension of a patio or outdoor entertainment space, but for little-used areas, choose low-water-use shrubs, not a lawn.

3 Efficient irrigation. Sprinklers are the least efficient method of irrigation because so much of the water evaporates before it hits the ground. They are the only effective way to water most lawns, however. Be sure the sprinklers are set so they water the lawn evenly and do not water any streets, sidewalks, walls, or other nongrowing objects. Plan to use a drip system on other areas.

4 Selecting low-water-use plants. Lists of various low-water-use plant are available at County Extension offices, the City of Albuquerque, the Rio Grande Botanic Garden, and other locations. Nurseries and garden centers can also help. Select plants that will fill the needs defined on the list and in the drawings, and group plants according to their water needs.

5 Soil improvement. Before any new landscape is installed, a soil test should be done. This will help determine soil needs. The required soil amendments should be added and thoroughly mixed with the soil before the plants are planted.

6 Mulching. Mulching helps hold the water in the soil so it can be used by the plant rather than evaporating. A mulch can be any covering on the ground, but an organic mulch will add nutrients to the soil as it breaks down.

7 Maintenance. All landscapes need to be maintained. If nothing more is required than picking out the trash that has blown in and occasionally pruning a plant back, pay attention to the landscape and do what needs to be done in a timely manner.

Because of the investment involved in the plants, install an inexpensive drip system even in the lowest water-use zones to water the plants the first two or three years, then gradually reduce the irrigation until the drip system can be removed. This will work only if the plants are selected to survive on natural rainfall in the area. Some plants native to the higher altitude areas or riverbanks of the region will need to be irrigated for their entire life cycle.

There are other ways to conserve water without changing the plants in the yard, and many plants other than cactus do not use large amounts of water. Quite a variety of plants, including trees, shrubs, flowers, and grasses, will use limited amounts of water without making the landscape appreciably different from a high-water-use landscape. Proper lawn irrigation can save more water than any other landscape measure. See chapter 3 for information on watering lawns.

If the yard is properly graded, the rainwater that falls on the yard will be retained for use by the plants rather than running off into the streets and arroyos to cause flooding somewhere else. A retention pond with a very permeable bottom, surrounded by the plants that use higher amounts of water, is an effective way of dealing with our uncertain rainfall.

JAPANESE GARDENS

Japanese rock gardens are closely associated with Zen Buddhism and the rituals and traditions of that practice, but a few basic principles can be explained here. Japanese garden design principles lend themselves to the conditions and plant material available in the Southwest and blend well with our architectural style. When Japanese landscapers set out to establish a rock or graveled area, they consider the ways it will be viewed. Generally the view is limited. Rarely is an entire garden visible at once or all the elements and designs in the garden viewed in the same way from different vantage points. Next, they plan the picture they want to present. Gravel and small rocks are frequently used to represent flowing water, while larger rocks represent cliffs or mountains. Mood is considered. How will viewing this garden from different vantage points affect the people who are viewing it? Elements are considered singly or in groups of three, five, or seven, and balance is very important. The gardens are not absolutely symmetrical, however. Absolute symmetry is boring, not pleasing to the eye. The asymmetrical balance of a Japanese garden is achieved by first assessing the visual weight of each element. Darker, larger, or course-textured objects tend to appear heavier, while lighter-colored, smaller, and fine-textured objects appear to be lighter. Once the visual weight of each object is determined, think of a teeter-totter. If a thin person is on one end and a heavy person on the other end, the thin person must be farther from the balance point than the heavy person. Each group of three objects should be grouped so that the center object—either rock or plant—is the fulcrum or balance point and the other objects are placed far enough from the fulcrum that they visually balance each other, the heavier one closer, the lighter one farther away. In groupings of more than three objects, use overlapping groupings of three to determine balance of objects. The groupings should be balanced in this way from very viewing angle. For a person more accustomed to Western symmetry than asymmetrical balance, this effect is difficult to achieve but apparent when it is achieved. A balanced arrangement of elements will create a soothing, harmonious effect rather than discord.

The art form, which is what rock gardens are in Japan, is developed as a discipline of the inner spirit for the purification of the mind and heart. The result is a strikingly effective arrangement of rocks totally unlike the dump truck piles we find here. Study and discipline are necessary to create an actual Zen rock garden. Any gardener, however, can apply one important principle: The entire garden and the effect it will have on people are considered before any rocks are placed on the ground.

DESIGNERS

For those who want help with landscape plants three types of highly skilled professionals are available: landscape architects, garden designers, and landscape contractors. A landscape architect is licensed by the state after completing university training and a rigorous test. Many landscape architects work with commercial landscapes, but some landscape architects specialize in home landscapes. A landscape architect may be needed if you have complex landscape quandaries. If you have a reasonable idea of what you want and do not have complicated drainage, irrigation, or grading problems to deal with, contact a garden designer. Garden designers may have more interest in home landscapes than a registered landscape architect, but they are not licensed by the state. Some garden designers have the same training as landscape architects but have not yet passed the registration exam, while others are talented individuals with less training. Landscape contractors install rather than design landscapes, but many landscape contractors employ landscape architects or designers to work with potential customers.

When interviewing professionals, ask to see a before-and-after portfolio of their projects; go see a completed project; and check their references. In residential projects, it is more important that you are pleased with the quality of their work and that they have strong references than that they hold a license.

Be frank about the amount of money you plan to spend on the project and the fee you expect to pay to the architect or designer. A fixed bid is generally the best way to control costs, but for a redesign project the designer might prefer a "time plus materials" arrangement. Ask for quick sketches of the project early in the process to determine if the landscape professional is going in the right direction. When the plan is completed and planting has begun, remember that a newly planted landscape may look a bit sparse until the plants begin to grow. However, the results in a few years will be more pleasing if the urge to overplant is avoided now.

LIGHTING

Outdoor lighting lost popularity when electricity became more expensive and energy conservation more important. Modern outdoor lighting is necessary for safety and security, and if it is designed effectively, can add drama to the yard without using much more energy than the porch and yard lights found at most homes. Most of the new outdoor lights are low-voltage lights that use less energy than the 120-volt lamps we use inside. These low-voltage lights require a transformer that usually comes with a prepackaged kit for outdoor lighting. Low-voltage lights can be used to spotlight plants in the garden. This is especially effective with trees with light-colored bark or interesting form. Low-voltage floodlights can light a patio or walkway so they can be used easily and safely at night. Globe and mushroom lights can illuminate ground covers, paths, stepping stones, and ponds.

Low-voltage lights are easy to install. With a little experimentation, you can create the effect you want. The idea is to see the light, not the fixture. Avoid glare by directing the lights away from the line of sight. Divide the yard into zones. The front zone might have medium-intensity light. In the center of the yard, install very low-intensity light to create an interplay of light and shadow, while the brightest light might be highlighting a focal point in the background. If you have difficulty with the design or want to create something extra special, you can contact a landscape designer or lighting specialist for assistance. Be sure the installation meets the National Electric Code. Most properly installed kits will meet the code, but do-it-yourself projects may not.

EDIBLE LANDSCAPING

Edible landscaping is a concept in which edible plants are mixed in with ornamental plants throughout the yard. Tomatoes can be grown in containers on the patio, lettuce or chives used to edge a flower bed, and fruit trees used as shade tress. Asparagus can be used as a background plant along a wall. If cosmos or some other large flower is planted just in front of the asparagus, it looks like a bouquet in the garden. Grapevines or annual vines like pole beans or cucumbers can be grown on a trellis to shade the south or west side of the house or a parking area. Sweet potatoes, mint, chamomile, or prostrate rosemary can be grown as a ground cover, replacing part of the lawn. Strawberries, small patio tomatoes, parsley, and many other attractive edible plants can be grown in hanging baskets. Many other combinations can make the yard productive as well as beautiful. If you do not limit yourself by thinking that vegetables have to be planted in rows and fruit in orchards, you can produce a variety of edible plants in any backyard.

FERNS

Ferns lend a cool, forestlike feel to the landscape but finding ferns to plant in a tree-shaded area that can withstand the cold winters, alkaline soils, and low humidity of southwestern gardens is difficult. If they are available, the species to buy are *Dryopteris erythrosora, Dryopteris filix-mas, Pellaea mucronata,* or *Pteridium aquilinum.* The common names for these species are Chinese wood fern, male fern, bird's foot fern, and bracken. Bracken grows wild in the mountains but is very difficult to transplant because of its deep root system. This same root system makes it difficult to eliminate once it is started in the yard, and it can be invasive, coming up in watered areas several feet away from where it was planted. Some other ferns will grow in shady areas of the Southwest if they are well watered and the soil has plenty of added organic matter. They would not, however, compete with surface-rooted trees like mulberry or elms.

Once you have planted the ferns under the tree, water them well and mulch the soil. Use a mixture of peat moss and fine wood chips or pine needles as a mulch to make the soil more acid and keep the soil moist.

FIRE PROTECTION

Appropriate landscaping can help protect forest homes from fire. The most important step is to remove dead or dry trees and brush from the property. Then fire-resistant plants can be planted. No plant will stop a full-fledged forest fire, but several plants are somewhat resistant to fire. These include yarrow, agave, mahonia, trumpet creeper, evergreen sumacs, prostrate rosemary, and the trunkless varieties of yucca.

All plants are more resistant to fire when they are green and growing than when they are dead and dry. If the mountain home is a vacation home, be sure everything planted around the house is drought tolerant so when the fire danger is highest there will still be live plants around the home.

WILDLIFE

Attracting wildlife, particularly birds, can add interest in the yard and is a common landscaping goal. Desert willow, penstemons, trumpet vine, honeysuckle, and other red or orange flowers will attract hummingbirds. Songbirds need a place to roost or nest, material with which to build a nest, and water and food in both winter and summer. Oregon grape holly, snowberry, Nanking cherry, female junipers, sagebrush, and elderberries are a few shrubs songbirds like. Sunflowers and sunflower-like flowers that produce abundant seeds are popular with songbirds too. Ornamental grasses will provide seeds for them over the winter. Near an open space the ornamental grasses will also attract quail and small mammals. The key to attracting large numbers of birds is variety. Plant as many different varieties as possible to feed the birds all year.

Be sure to provide water as well as food for the birds. A birdbath or small pond with rocks for the birds to perch on will attract more birds. A pond is also a good place to have fish, frogs, turtles, and water plants.

CHAPTER 3

Irrigation

LAWNS

In the arid and semiarid climate of the Southwest almost all landscape plants must be irrigated. Because our water reserves are limited, irrigating efficiently is very important. The most important aspect of irrigating efficiently is to make sure the irrigation system is operating properly. Sprinklers and flood irrigation are the least efficient means of irrigation, but they are the only effective way to irrigate a lawn. To avoid misuse of water on the lawn, make sure sprinklers are properly adjusted. A cloud of mist indicates an improperly adjusted sprinkler. Most sprinklers have a screw adjustment on top that allows the droplet size to be adjusted. Determine if sprinklers are watering evenly by placing cans on the lawn at different locations and measuring the amount of water in each can after fifteen minutes. If the amounts in the cans vary a great deal even with the sprinkler heads adjusted properly, a new sprinkler system may be in order.

Uneven watering can waste water because the entire lawn must be watered until the driest spot is wet enough to support the growth of the grass. To refurbish an old sprinkler system, all the heads will need to be replaced, but the pipes may not. In any sprinkler system the sprinkler heads need to be the same type and to have the same degree of wear in order for the lawn to be watered evenly. The pipes can be plastic, galvanized metal, or copper. To decide if they should be replaced, check for leaks by searching for wet spots in the soil. If there is an area where the grass is always greener, the pipes may be leaking there. Dig a hole or probe the soil to be sure it is not soggy. Next check to be sure water is coming out of all the sprinkler heads. If it is not, the pipes may be clogged. If any part of the pipe is either clogged or leaking it is advisable to replace all the pipes if they are several years old.

Next, measure the size of the pipe and the spacing between the current heads. Go to a sprinkler dealer and ask what types of heads will work with that size pipe at that spacing. If you can find sprinkler heads that will work with the existing system and that can be properly connected to the existing pipes, the pipes do not have to be replaced. Compare the price and expected life of the new sprinkler heads with an entirely new system. If the pipes do not have to be replaced, remove the heads very carefully. If the pipes are damaged during removal, the entire system must be replaced.

Be sure the sprinklers water only the lawn and not streets, sidewalks, or houses. In Albuquerque homeowners can be fined for allowing water to run into the street. In any case, such watering is wasteful and will become increasingly expensive. Many people overwater lawns. The best way to water the lawn is to put enough water on the lawn so it soaks in eight to twelve inches; put on only one to two inches per week. The number of inches applied can be determined by the can method described above.

More lawn problems are caused by improper watering than by any disease or insect problem. Soil preparation may cause watering problems if a layer of topsoil or soil conditioner was put on top of sandy soil then sod was laid over that. The surface of each layer presents a barrier to root and water penetration. The roots of the grass and the water spread along the undersurface of the sod. If they manage to penetrate the conditioner or topsoil, they spread through that layer before penetrating the sand underneath. When preparing to lay sod, be sure to mix organic matter into the top eight inches of the soil rather than putting it in a layer on top and laying sod over it. If an established lawn requires constant watering because it was prepared in layers, the situation can be improved by deep power raking or coring in spring and fall, then topdressing with sand similar to the sandy soil underneath. Several treatments over a period of years will be required to remove the effects of the layering.

Consistent, uniform irrigation is essential to the production of high-quality lawns. Proper irrigation is not easy. To determine when to water, walk across the lawn in the cooler parts of the day. If three or four footprints are still visible after each step, it is time to water. Another way is to use a probe. Push a large screwdriver or knitting needle into the soil until it stops. It will stop when it has reached dry soil. If it stops before penetrating six inches, it is time to water.

The amount of water to apply depends on the moisture in the soil, the infiltration rate, and the ability of the soil to retain water. Apply enough water to reach the entire root zone of the grass. Use a probe to determine how much water is needed to penetrate eight to twelve inches into the soil.

Only the frequency should change from season to season. To check the penetration of the water, turn the sprinklers on for five minutes. Twenty-four hours later dig a test hole to find out how far the water penetrated. Use that number to figure out how long to water. Divide that number into sixty to determine the number of minutes to water. For example, if the water penetrated four inches, water fifteen minutes each time. If it penetrated only two inches, water thirty minutes each time. In winter, water once a month for the same length of time as in the summer.

Calculating Irrigation Depth

Turn sprinklers on for 5 minutes.

Dig a test hole to find out how far the water penetrated.

Divide that number into 60 to determine the number of minutes to water

Example:

Water penetration = 4 inches

60/4 = 15 minutes

Be sure the temperature is above freezing when watering in winter so the hose, sprinklers, and faucets do not freeze.

Water will infiltrate sand much more quickly than it will clay, but the clay will retain the water for a longer period of time. A lawn in sandy soil may need an inch of water every third day, while on a clay soil it may need two inches of water once a week. Do not apply water more quickly than it can penetrate the soil. On a clay soil, water should be applied from sprinklers with low output. A few sprinklers will put out water faster than it can infiltrate into even sandy soil. Thatch will also affect the infiltration rate of the soil. If water does not infiltrate the soil as quickly as it should because of a thatch layer or impenetrable sod surface, sprinkle it for about fifteen minutes to moisten the surface, wait about half an hour then sprinkle again to apply as much water as the grass needs. Do not overwater the lawn. Watering too frequently reduces soil oxygen; restricts root growth; increases soil compaction, nutrient loss by leaching, and fungus attacks; and decreases overall turf vigor.

By starting in early spring, you can condition grass to survive periods with less water during the summer. The most important factor is the watering schedule. Water only when necessary. Avoid frequent, shallow waterings. Have the soil analyzed, especially for potassium. High levels of potassium help grass resist drought stress. Many southwestern soils have naturally high potassium levels, but after several years the grass will use all the potassium that was there to start with. If the soil does not have high potassium levels, apply a high potassium fertilizer. See chapter 1 for information on soil testing.

PLANTINGS

The most efficient way to irrigate landscapes, flower beds, and gardens is with a drip system. Drip emitters come in one-, two-, and five-gallon-per-hour (gph) sizes. The amount of water a plant needs depends on a number of factors. Use the following table to determine how many emitters to use. Determine how long it takes the water from the emitters to soak into the ground one foot by using a probe or digging a hole. Water for that length of time for annuals and perennials, twice that long for shrubs, and three times that long for trees. The length of time depends on the soil type. For perennial and annual flowers, use one emitter per plant. For shrubs, flowers, or grass planted under trees, use emitters for the trees and an appropriate system for the other plants as well. The number of times to water will vary with the season. Water at least once in December, January, and February; one or two times a week in March through May as well as September through November; and three to four times a week in June, July, and August. Distributors will provide specific instructions on designing, installing, and operating their systems. Be sure to check the emitters and filters frequently to make sure they are not clogged.

Drip systems require frequent checking and maintenance. If that is not possible, a bubbler distribu-

DRIP TARGETS

What kind of emitter? How many? Where?

LOW SHRUBS 2 TO 3 FEET TALL
One or two 1-gph emitters, placed 6 to 12 inches from base of plant

SHRUBS, TREES TO 5 FEET TALL
Two or three 1-gph emitters placed a foot away from base of plant

SHRUBS, TREES 5 TO 10 FEET TALL
Three or four 1-gph emitters (or one or two 2-gph emitters) equally spaced around the plant, $1^1/_2$ to 2 feet from trunk

TREES 10 TO 20 FEET TALL
Four to six 1-gph emitters (or two or three 2-gph emitters) equally spaced around drip line

TREES OVER 20 FEET TALL
Six to twelve 1-gph emitters (or three to six 2-gph emitters) equally spaced around drip line

GROUND COVERS, fIOWERS
Enough 1 gph emitters to make 100% wetted area:
—for light sandy soil, space 1 to $1^1/_2$ feet apart
—for medium loam, space 2 feet apart
—for heavy clay soil, space $2^1/_2$ ft apart
-or use perforated tubing laid in parallel rows

VEGETABLE GARDENS
Row crops
Use $^1/_2$- or 1-gph emitters closely spaced (as for ground covers above) on a line or perforated tubing with holes 12 to 18 inches apart

Widely spaced plants (squash, tomatoes)
One to four 1-gph emitters at each plant

POTTED PLANTS
Use one $^1/_2$- or 1-gph emitters per pot (depending on size of container) on extension tubes, or overhead mister turned on more frequently for short periods

Use this chart only as a guide, keeping in mind different plant needs, growing conditions, and watering times. Most manufacturers base emitter flow rates on a working pressure of 15 to 20 pounds per square inch (psi). At higher water pressures, the actual flow increases accordingly.

tion system with a timer can be set to water from every few days to once a week. A bubbler system with the appropriate timer will be more expensive than most drip systems but also more reliable. Be sure the surface is graded properly and the bubblers run slowly enough to allow the water to soak into the soil. Experiment with the soil to see how long it takes the water to soak in to a depth of eighteen inches and how long it stays moist at a depth of six inches. Set the timer so it will water every time the soil dries to a depth of six inches. This will depend on the expected weather. Plants need the most water in the hot, windy months of May, June, and July. Increase the frequency of watering if you go on vacation during those months. As the seasons change, do not change the length of watering time, just the frequency.

The low humidity, cold weather, and winds of southwestern winters can dehydrate plants even when they are dormant. Lawns and evergreen trees should be watered every month or so in winter. Water newly planted deciduous trees every two weeks. Established deciduous trees should be watered two or three times between the time they drop their leaves and the time the buds begin to swell. The roots need to be protected from dehydration. Heavy snows reduce the need to water; high winds increase the need. Apply about an inch of water each time. Be sure the temperature is above freezing to avoid damaging hoses, sprinklers, faucets, and valves and to prevent ice from forming on the branches of trees. Be especially careful that water does not run off the lawn and onto the sidewalk or street, as it may freeze when night comes and cause accidents. After watering, disconnect the hoses, drain all the water from them, and put them back in storage.

Summer watering during the rainy season is also very important. Most thundershowers provide less than an inch of rain, and those that are more than an inch frequently fall so rapidly that less than an inch of water soaks into the lawn. A lawn can use up to two to three inches of water per week, depending on grass type grass and how much sun the lawn gets.

When an inch of rain falls over a period of more than an hour, wait for three days to water the lawn. If two or more inches fall over a period of more than three hours, wait for a week to water, unless the soil is sandy. Sandy soil dries out quickly and should be watered again within three days no matter how much water it gets. If a shower of more than a third of an inch falls on the lawn, skip watering for one day and resume on the normal schedule the next day. Check the rainfall with a rain gauge or straight-sided container in your own yard. Do not rely on weather service reports of amounts at the airport or maximum amounts in different areas of the city. Rainfall amounts can vary within a mile or less in the Southwest.

Some plants should never be watered with sprinklers. Sprinkling the roses may do them more harm than good. Roses are susceptible to many diseases that are more likely to occur if the leaves are wet and the humidity high. Roses are much better off with a properly designed drip system. A drip system is less expensive than a sprinkler system, although it will have to be replaced sooner. It can cut water use in half when compared to sprinklers, and the roses will be healthier. (See chapter 8 for a full discussion of roses.)

CHAPTER 4

Lawns and Ornamental Grasses

TYPES OF GRASS

Grasses are classified according to the temperatures at which they grow best. Cool-season grasses grow best at temperatures between about 50 and 80°F. The most common cool-season lawn grasses are bluegrass, fescue, and ryegrass. In much of the Southwest cool-season grasses have a short growing season in the spring, go dormant for the summer, then have a longer growing season in the fall. Warm-season grasses grow best when temperatures are above 80°F. The most common warm-season grass in the Southwest is Bermuda. Native buffalo grass and blue grama are also warm-season grasses. Zoysia is a transition-zone grass. It continues to grow in slightly cooler weather than warm-season grasses and slightly warmer weather than cool-season. It does extremely well in the transition zone in the eastern part of the United States but less well in the soil and low humidity of the Southwest.

PLANTING

The type of grass to plant depends on how the lawn will be used and where it is in relation to the house and trees. Cool-season grasses are best for high-elevation areas; warm-season grasses, for low elevations. Much of the region is in the transition zone where either will work. In shade, the cool-season grasses are the best choice. Some of the new, fine-bladed fescues are rather drought tolerant, although their longer growing season requires irrigation and mowing early in the spring and late in the fall. Find out from a local nursery what is available, then ask to see lawns they have installed to determine how well the variety will do in different situations. Bermuda is best for a thick, soft lawn for children to play on in summer. Some of the hybrid Bermudas are less invasive than common Bermuda. Bluegrass and fescue can take more wear and tear in the winter because they keep growing longer than Bermuda grass. However they also require more water and care, especially bluegrass.

For a minimum-care lawn in a large area, try buffalo grass. It will take as much water to establish as it takes to establish other lawns, but water can be reduced once the buffalo grass starts to fill in and it doesn't have to be mowed too often. Because the buffalo grass will be growing as a lawn not a pasture, prepare the soil the same as for any other lawn. Buffalo grass takes a long time to become well established, so it is particularly important to control any weeds in the area.

Start by tilling the entire area to be planted. Tillers can be rented from most equipment rental outlets. If the soil is hard and compacted, water the area the day before tilling. If in-ground sprinklers are already in place, remove the grass from around each sprinkler head before tilling and keep the tiller away from the sprinklers. A tall flag next to each sprinkler head will help the tiller operator avoid the heads.

Mix some organic matter with the surface soil while tilling. Phosphate or potassium fertilizer may also be added if a soil test indicates it is needed.

SUMMARY OF GRASS ATTRIBUTES

GRASS TYPE	WATER USE	PLANTING TIME	SEEDING RATE (PER 100 SQ. FT.)	MOWING HEIGHT
Bluegrass	High	September or March	2–3 lb.	2–3"
Tall fescue	Medium–High	September or March	6–8 lb.	$2^{1}/_{2}$–$3^{1}/_{2}$"
Ryegrass	Medium–High	September or March	5–6 lb.	2–3"
Zoysia	Medium	April	not generally seeded	$1^{1}/_{2}$–2"
Bermuda	Medium	May	not generally seeded	$^{3}/_{4}$–$1^{1}/_{2}$"
Buffalo grass	Low	June–July	2 lb. live seed	2–$2^{1}/_{2}$"
Blue gramma	Low	June–July	3–5lb.	2–$2^{1}/_{2}$"

Rake out stones and clumps of roots and level the soil. Water the area to get weeds to sprout then kill the weeds either with herbicides or another tilling operation. If a herbicide is used, make sure it has a short waiting period between spraying and planting. Do not plant before the end of the waiting period. Install sprinklers if necessary, then level the soil. Make sure the soil is finely pulverized, not

Cool Season Grasses
Kentucky bluegrass
Tall fescue
Ryegrass

Warm Season Grasses
Bermuda
Buffalo
Blue Gramma

Transition Zone Grass
Zoysia

crusty or full of clods. Either roll out sod or scatter seed at the rate described on the package for new lawns. The regular seeding rate per one thousand square feet for bluegrass is 2 to 3 pounds; tall fescue, 6 to 8 pounds; ryegrass, 5 to 6 pounds. The amount of seed to buy depends on the percentage of live seed. This will usually be around 70 to 80 percent. Buffalo grass seeds grow in little burs. Untreated burs have about 50 percent live seed and 50 percent other material. Buffalo grass seed with a large percentage of live seed will be considerably more expensive because of the treatment process that removes some of the burs. The seeding rate for Buffalo grass is about 2 pounds live seed per 1,000 square feet. If the seed is 50 percent live seed, 4 pounds per thousand square feet must be planted. Compare price and percentage of live seed to determine what seed to buy.

Use a rotary or drop-type grass seeder rather than sowing the seed by hand. Be sure the seeder is set to apply the correct amount. Press the seed into the soil with boards or a roller after planting to be sure all the seed is in contact with soil. Apply a slow-release starter fertilizer during seeding to insure rapid establishment. Avoid water soluble fertilizers as too much fertilizer will burn the new seedlings. In about four to six weeks, fertilize again. Water immediately after seeding or rolling out sod. Water sod daily for the first two weeks, then gradually establish a normal watering schedule for that grass type and season. After the first watering, the seedbed should never be allowed to dry out until the seeds have germinated. If the seeds ever become dry, all the work and expense will have been in vain. Water gently so germinating seedlings are not dislodged or washed around.

Early fall or spring is the best time for renewing thin or spotty bluegrass or fescue lawns. Before scattering expensive seed, take time to correct the conditions that caused the problem. The lawn may be thin or spotty for several reasons. Among these are poor soil, thatch more than half an inch thick, weather stress, attack by diseases or insects, selection of the wrong type or varieties of grass, and improper care. Some soil problems may require the removal of the lawn and complete renovation starting with the soil rather than overseeding. Sod may have been laid over a compacted or poorly prepared soil, thus preventing the roots of the sod from penetrating the soil. Shallow rooting can also be a problem in lawns that are watered frequently and shallowly. Learn correct watering, mowing, and fertilizing techniques before renovating a lawn or the same problems will recur.

Do not use crabgrass preventers or broadleaf weed killers for one month before overseeding. Mow existing grass short (one and a half inches) to keep grass and weeds from competing with the new seedlings. Use a grass catcher on the mower or rake up grass clippings. Do not scalp off vegetation. Some is needed to protect the germinating seed from the wind and sun.

To get the seed to the soil, cut through the remaining vegetation. For very small areas, a heavy garden rake can be used to expose the soil in bare spots. A power rake, available for rent at nurseries and rental agencies, can also be used. Choose a heavy duty machine with solid, thin blades (one-sixteenth to one-eighth inch). Thick blades damage the turf and beat, rather than slice, the soil. Set the rake to slice one-eighth to one-quarter inch into the soil. Power rake in two directions at right angles to each other. The soil should be moist but not soggy.

On heavy clay or compacted soils a core aerator can be used. This pulls plugs from the soil and gives the new seed a place to germinate. Go over the turf three to five times with a core aerator. Sow seed at about half the rate for new lawns. Rake lightly after seeding or use a lightweight roller to make sure the soil is in contact with the seed. Daily watering will be necessary at first, then gradually return to the regular watering schedule. Mow as soon as the grass is three inches tall, with the mower set at two inches.

Clover and other legumes take nitrogen from the air and put it into the soil. Before chemical fertilizers were used, legumes were planted in lawns to fertilize them and reduce the need to apply manure. Chemical fertilizers have now replaced both legumes and manure on most lawns. Clover will still provide nitrogen for the grass, but it is a different tex-ture and slightly different color from many lawn grasses and grows at a different rate so the lawn looks patchy. Under certain conditions the clover can take over the lawn, eliminating the grass. In an informal or low-maintenance lawn, clover is a good idea, but it is not generally used in formal lawn situations.

MOWING

Mowing height depends on time of year and the type of lawn. Cool-sea-son lawns, such as bluegrass and fescue, should be allowed to remain taller than warm-season grasses like Bermuda and buffalo grass. Lawns should be allowed to grow a little taller during hot weather. Bluegrass and rye-grass can be mowed to two inches in spring and fall but should be allowed to grow to three inches in the summer. Tall fescue should be allowed to grow to three and a half inches in summer and can be cut to two and a half inches in spring and fall. Bermuda grass can be cut to one and a half inches year-round, and buffalo grass can be cut to two inches year-round.

If the grass is allowed to grow a little taller, it will be healthier and more drought resistant.

If grass has been allowed to go for a few weeks without mowing and is significantly taller than the recommended mowing height, do not cut it to the recommended height all at once. Never cut off more than one-third of the blade of the grass. For example, if Bermuda grass is six inches tall, cut it to four inches if the lawn mower can be set that high, or to the highest setting of the mower. Water the grass, and about three days later cut it to just below three inches, then three or four days later, after another watering, cut it to the recommended height. More frequent mowing makes the lawn healthier, so once the lawn is the recommended height, try to mow frequently enough to avoid having to cut too much off at once.

The best thing to do with lawn clippings is to leave them on the lawn. Clippings do not contribute to thatch. Thatch is caused by overfertilizing and overwatering. The clippings decompose easily and return fertilizer to the soil. Leaving the grass clippings on the soil can reduce the fertilizer needs by as much as 25 percent. It can also reduce the amount of time it takes to mow the lawn. To avoid making the lawn look unattractive because the clippings are sitting on top of the grass, mow more often. Set the lawn mower at the highest setting for the grass type, then mow it every time it grows one inch. This will be more often at some times of year than others. In late spring and early fall, cool-season lawns will probably have to be mowed every three or four days unless they are stressed for water or fertilizer. If the clippings must be removed from the lawn, use them as mulch for other parts of the yard. They will help keep the soil cool, reduce weed growth, and add fertility to the soil. Spread all the clippings out in a thin layer over the entire area to be mulched rather than piling them too deep. A thick layer of clippings can smell bad as they rot, and a large pile of clippings can start fire from the heat that builds up during the decomposition. Once the first layer of clippings has dried, put a fresh layer on top. Do not use Bermuda grass clippings as mulch. Any little stem section in the Bermuda grass will start to grow and the grass will soon take over the mulched area.

FERTILIZING

Do not fertilize a lawn in the spring until it shows a touch of green. The nitrogen in most lawn fertilizers is water soluble, and if it is put on too early, it will wash away before the grass has a chance to use it. Different varieties of grass will begin to turn green at different times. Don't get impatient with Bermuda grass. Adding fertilizer will not make it turn green sooner. It is waiting for the weather to get thoroughly warm. Bermuda grass that is not heavily used can be fertilized with one pound of nitrogen per one thousand square feet in May. If it gets heavier use, it can be fertilized again in July.

Cool-season grasses should be fertilized in the fall. Do not fertilize Bermuda grass or buffalo grass then. Fall fertilizing of bluegrass, fescue, or ryegrass stimulates root growth more than top growth and builds energy reserves in the grass plants so they will green up earlier in the spring. It also reduces summer "burnout" and is less likely to promote weed and disease problems. A low-maintenance schedule for a cool-season lawn is to fertilize it once a year, in September. For better growth and a greener lawn over a longer period of time, fertilize in September, November, and May. Use a fertilizer containing both slow-release and water soluble fertilizers in September. In November use water soluble fertilizer only, and in May, use slow-release fertilizer only. Apply one to one and a half pounds of nitrogen per one thousand square feet each time. The first number of the analysis on the bag tells the percentage of nitrogen in the fertilizer. If a fertilizer has 20 percent nitrogen, five pounds of the fertilizer will provide one pound of nitrogen. If it has 30 percent nitrogen, use three pounds of fertilizer per one thousand square feet to provide one pound of nitrogen.

Buffalo grass will turn brown if it is overfertilized, but a little fertilizer once a year will help it grow fast enough to recover from use. Water it just enough to keep it from turning brown and mowing will be required only a few times a year. If the lawn is heavily used, water a little more to allow the grass to recover quickly. Read the directions on the fertilizer bag and put slightly less fertilizer on than is recommended. Be sure to water the lawn well after fertilizing so the fertilizer is washed into the soil where the plant roots can use it.

Lawns on highly alkaline soils may turn yellow, a condition known as iron chlorosis. There may be iron in the soil but it is not available because of the alkalinity. Iron deficiencies can be corrected by applying iron sulfates or iron chelates. Apply iron chelates as directed on the label. Dissolve iron sulfate in water at the rate of one pound of the chemical in twenty-five gallons of water. (A stronger solution could burn the grass.) Apply twelve and a half gallons of the solution to one thousand square feet of lawn.

THATCH

Whether to dethatch or aerate depends on the lawn's problems. Dethatching will take care of a thatch layer and aeration will relieve surface compaction. A lawn with more than three-quarters of an inch of thatch needs to be dethatched. Thatch is a layer of dead root and stem tissue on the surface of the soil. It forms a spongy layer so the grass feels springy underfoot. The grass roots grow into the thatch rather than into the soil, making the grass more susceptible to drought, disease, and insect attack. It also prevents good water penetration. Lawns with a heavy thatch layer may need to be watered every day to keep them green. The best time to dethatch is just before a major period of growth. Dethatch Bermuda grass lawns any time before the middle of August. Bluegrass lawns should be dethatched either in early spring, just as they are getting green, or in early fall just as the weather starts to cool off. Once the thatch has been removed, keep from forming new thatch on bluegrass lawns through proper lawn management as described above.

Bermuda grass and zoysia grass build up heavy thatch layers that must be removed on a regular basis no matter what management practices are used. Less frequent watering and more frequent mowing will slow the thatch buildup. Fertilize only once a year, at the beginning of summer, to help keep thatch to a minimum.

Compacted soils may need to be aerated. Any soil can become compacted but some are more likely to compact than others. Soils with particles of uniform size are likely to compact. A uniform sand or a clay soil will become compacted more easily than loam soil with mixed particle sizes. Heavily used grass areas become compacted easily. Athletic fields and parks need frequent aeration. Home yards have fewer compaction problems. A yard where all the neighborhood children play may need to be aerated once or twice a year. If no one walks on the lawn except to mow it, it should never need to be aerated.

Surface compaction can be taken care of with a core aerator, a machine that takes little plugs of grass and soil out of the lawn and puts them on top. These can then be broken up and raked loosely back into the holes so water and oxygen can penetrate easily. This also helps reduce thatch somewhat by raking soil down into the thatch layer and covering some thatch, but the main purpose of aeration is to allow water and oxygen to enter compacted soil. Solid-tine aerators or pushing a gardening fork into the lawn further compacts the soil on the edges of the holes so that water cannot penetrate easily even though there are holes in the lawn. A core aerator is the best choice for effectively eliminating surface compaction.

Deep soil compaction, or hardpan, can be present in native soils or can be caused by heavy equipment operation. In fields where hardpan is a problem, a type of plow called a subsoiler can be used to cut through the hardpan. A subsoiler has blades that cut through the soil from several inches to four feet below the surface to break up a hardpan. It must be pulled by a large tractor, which makes it impractical to operate one in the average yard. A more practical way of dealing with a hardpan in a yard is to try to break through it when planting a tree or shrub, but otherwise leave the hardpan intact and water carefully to avoid wasting water.

DISEASE AND INSECTS

Fungus can be a problem in bluegrass at any time of the year. Conditions that favor most fungal diseases are high humidity, warm temperatures, and grass that has recently been stressed. A few fungi prefer cool temperatures rather than warm. The best preventative is proper lawn care.

Round brown patches in the lawn are indicative of the fungal disease called brown patch, but lawn fungal diseases cannot be positively identified without examining the fungal fruiting bodies under a microscope. Brown patch is a disease that attacks lawns that have been over-fertilized and overwatered. Irregular circular areas in a lawn, a few inches to several feet in diameter, may turn brown and die. Avoid problems by watering lawns early in the day to give the grass time to dry out before night. If the disease is severe, apply a fungicide. Dollar spot causes small, round, dead spots about the size of a silver dollar. Use the same preventative measures as for brown spot. Pythium blight, sometimes called grease spot, is also a fungus disease. Early in the morning there may be circular spots, two inches in diameter, surrounded by blackened grass blades that are intertwined with fungal threads. Pythium is very fast acting and can kill grass within twenty-four hours. The grass lies flat on the ground after it has been killed. Most general purpose fungicides do little to control pythium. Select a fungicide recommended for pythium blight.

Treat fungal problems immediately. A number of effective lawn fungicides are available, but they do not all control the same fungus. Chemical controls for brown patch or dollar spot are fungicides containing the active ingredient chlorothalonil. Use benomyl, iprodione, or methyl thiophanate for fusarium and chloroneb or ethazole on pythium.

Fairy ring is a fungus that grows in continually wider rings from a central area, usually a rotting tree stump or other source. Each year a mass of fungal mycelial growth spreads outward into new soil. This growth matures and produces mushrooms, then dies and breaks down. In the area where mycelial growth is taking place, the fungus uses all the available nutrients and moisture. The white stringy growth is so thick the soil becomes very solid and compacted. This sometimes kills the grass. The only way to eliminate the fungus is to till up the entire area, mix the infected soil thoroughly with uninfected soil, and replant the lawn. Generally it is not worth the effort. As the fungus starts to break down on the inside of the ring the nutrients are released to the grass again. The soil becomes looser and more aerated so water can penetrate more easily. In a lawn that is not heavily fertilized, the area just inside the fairy ring will be the most fertile part of the lawn and therefore will turn green earlier. The effect is not as noticeable in heavily fertilized lawns.

Decaying tree stumps or roots can produce various types of mushrooms. Unless small children or pets are likely to eat mushrooms that come up in the lawn, there is no reason to get rid of them. The decay process will enrich the soil, and the tree roots won't have to be removed by digging or chopping them out to plant something else there.

If small children or pets frequently play in the yard, pick the mushrooms each day before letting the child or pet into the yard. There are no chemical controls for use in the backyard, so manually removing the mushrooms or the fungal fibers underground is the only means of control.

The most common insect problem in lawns is grubs. Two types of white grublike insect larvae may be in a lawn: the common white grub and the Denver billbug. Both can be present in large numbers without doing severe damage if the lawn is well cared for.

Common white grubs are fat, wormlike insects with little stubby legs. They grow up to be May or June beetles. These are fat, tan or brownish beetles that are attracted to light. They will gather under the porch light or on the screen door in late spring and early summer if their numbers are large. They have one generation per year. After the adults emerge from the ground they lay their eggs in the lawn, the eggs hatch, and the larvae start feeding. The larvae overwinter deep in the soil, return to the root zone in early spring to feed for a few more weeks, then pupate deeper in the soil until later in the spring or summer. In the spring these grubs are almost impossible to control and should be left alone unless very high numbers are present. High numbers means about twenty to thirty grubs per square foot.

The best time to control the common white grub is just after the grub hatches from the egg. This happens in late July or early August. If grub populations are around fifteen to twenty per square foot, apply some control measures at that time. One well-timed, effective spray will prevent the need for additional applications for white grubs. In sensitive areas, parasitic nematodes (but *not* Milky Spore) are an option, but control may be slow and incomplete.

The billbug larvae are smaller, legless larvae with brown heads. They are about one-third to one-half inch long. Billbugs grow up to be dark, gray-black snout beetles, about one-third to one-half inch long. Denver billbugs have light-colored markings on their back. Except for the light-colored markings they look like large flour weevils. The adults can often be found crawling on masonry and across sidewalks next to lawns in late spring and summer. Although adults feed on the lawn, most of the damage is caused by the larval stage, which cannot be effectively controlled by insecticides. Treatments should be timed for periods of peak adult activity. This peak generally occurs during June or July. If adult billbugs are readily observed on sidewalks and driveways, control may be called for. The same insecticides recommended above, including the proper species of parasitic nematodes, will control adult billbugs.

WEEDS

Many types of broadleaf weeds can invade a lawn. These can generally be controlled by appropriate maintenance practices that favor the lawn grass over the weeds or by using broadleaf weed killers. Broadleaf weed killers can harm trees and other ornamental plants whose roots penetrate the lawn area, so they should be used with extreme care. Unless the weeds are strongly established, most of them can be crowded out by the grass if it is mowed, watered, and fertilized correctly. Once large numbers of

> **Common Pollen Sources**
> **All grasses**
> **Weeds**
> careless weed
> ragweed
> pigweed
> kochia
> tumbleweed

weeds become established, especially perennial or large-rooted weeds like dandelion, they may have to be pulled or dug out.

Spurge and crabgrass are more difficult to kill than many other weeds. If the plants are already producing seeds, the best solution is to pull out the plant and destroy it. Find the root at the center of the plant and try to pull up the entire plant. This will limit the seeds in the lawn.

If chemical solutions are preferred, buy a pesticide that is particularly formulated for the weed that is there. If a preemergent herbicide is applied in the spring, a herbicide may need to be reapplied in early summer the next year. Spurge is a very difficult weed to eradicate once it has gone to seed. Keep the lawn as healthy as possible so it can compete effectively with the spurge when it does appear.

Bermuda grass can become a weed in a cool-season lawn, and it is very difficult to eliminate. In colder areas, fall watering and fertilizing can make the Bermuda grass very succulent and susceptible to freezing out in the winter. In the transition zone, where both cool- and warm-season grasses will grow, there are no effective cultural practices. The most effective method is to use herbicides to kill the Bermuda grass, then reseed the area with bluegrass. The best time to do that is in late summer. In late August, when the Bermuda grass is growing well, apply glyphosate herbicide according to the directions. Wait about two weeks until the Bermuda grass is dead, then dig it out or till up the area, prepare a smooth seedbed, and plant bluegrass seed. Keep the seed moist until the grass comes up. When it is about three inches high, start treating the new area like the rest of the lawn.

To keep the Bermuda grass from spreading during the summer, apply glyphosate as soon as it is thoroughly green. Bluegrass seed will not germinate well in the summer, so it will be difficult to reestablish bluegrass in the area until fall. If the Bermuda grass is killed in summer, other weeds could invade the area. To encourage the bluegrass to outcompete the Bermuda grass, put a slow-release fertilizer on in early spring then do not fertilize for the rest of the summer. Mow at a height of two and a half inches and keep the lawn well watered to a depth of eight inches all summer.

REPLACING LAWNS WITH GROUND COVER

If grass is not needed for a sitting area or playing field, lower water-use ground covers can be used. Some ground covers for light shade include dwarf plumbago, creeping potentilla, vinca minor, and ajuga. Thyme, creeping rosemary, iceplant, desert zinnia, and many others can be used in full sun. To convert a lawn to a ground cover, kill off the lawn by spraying it with glyphosate. This should be done in the early fall or spring for bluegrass and in late summer for Bermuda grass. If the grass is higher than the sidewalk or curb around it, strip the sod and remove it to lower the surface. Otherwise, till the grass into the soil, although for best results Bermuda grass should be removed even after spraying. Make any changes needed to the irrigation system. Water use can be reduced by using drip tubing or leaky pipe for low-water-use ground covers. Plant the ground covers about eighteen inches apart in a diamond pattern and water them thoroughly. Most ground covers will fill in within a season or two and produce a lower water alternative to the lawn.

ORNAMENTAL GRASSES

The use of ornamental grasses in the home landscape has seen a significant increase in recent years as new varieties have been developed and people have realized how attractive they can be in all seasons of the year. For the rock garden, try bulbous oat grass, blue fescue, blue oat grass, purple moor grass, or Indian rice grass. Bulbous oat grass grows to one and a half to two feet tall and is most attractive in early spring and late fall. It can be cut back in midsummer. Blue fescue is one of the most common and attractive ornamental grasses. It forms low clumps, and some of the variants have extremely blue foliage. It remains attractive through the winter. Blue oat grass grows to three feet and has attractive, distinctive foliage. Purple moor grass has yellow-and-green striped foliage and yellow, green, and purple flowers in the summer. Indian rice grass is a native New Mexico plant that has a fine texture and is attractive all winter. It grows one to two feet tall.

As specimen plants, feather reed grass, weeping love grass, Chinese silver grass, maiden grass, striped eulalia grass, zebra grass, fountain grass, and ribbon grass can be used. Of these, Chinese silver grass is the tallest, although it is not as wide spreading a plant as some of the others. Maiden grass, striped eulalia grass, zebra grass, and feather reed grass all have upright forms and grow to three to six feet. Ribbon grass has an upright open form although it reaches only about four feet. Weeping love grass and fountain grass form mounds, with the seed heads extending above the foliage.

Ornamental grasses usually require minimal care throughout the growing season. Make sure they get adequate water, but do not waterlog the soil. Nitrogen fertilizer will help produce attractive foliage. It should be applied just as the foliage begins to grow in the spring, again in midsummer, and in late fall for those grasses that remain green until late in the season. Because many of the grasses are most attractive in late fall, division and cutting back should be left until early spring. Perennial grasses should be divided every seven to ten years, or sooner if growth is occurring only around the outer edges. After division, they can be replanted in the same place if organic matter and fertilizers have been added to the soil. The plants should be cut back to within six inches of the ground early each spring, before they begin to grow.

Bamboo is one of the largest and best-known ornamental grasses. There are two distinct types of bamboo, running and clumping. Several of the running types and a few clumping types are hardy to our normal low temperatures. Running types will spread vigorously and can cover a large area in a short period of time. They can be difficult to contain and can cause damage to sidewalks and retaining walls. Clumping bamboos, on the other hand, spread only a short distance.

Bamboos that are hardy to 0°F include simon, golden, giant timber, black, arrow, palmate, and fountain bamboo. Bamboos that are hardy to minus 20°F include yellow grove bamboo and the rare species *Thamnocalamus spathaceus*. Fountain bamboo and *Thamnocalamus spathaceus* are the only clumping varieties of those listed. All the listed varieties can get to at least ten feet tall with adequate water and fertilization. Some, like the giant timber bamboo, can get much taller.

The best way to contain bamboo is to put a barrier around it so the roots cannot spread. The roots are rather shallow so the barrier only needs to be about eighteen inches deep. Plant the bamboo in a bucket or other container with the bottom removed so water can drain out, or dig a trench and put a fiberglass or metal barrier in the trench. Any joints in the metal or fiberglass should be joined tightly so the roots cannot separate the pieces and grow through. Do not count on a wall between neighboring yards to contain bamboo. Wall footings generally do not go deep enough, and the bamboo could grow under the wall and spread into the neighbor's yard. Rapidly growing bamboo can also knock down retaining walls and other rock work if the roots are not separated from the wall with a continuous in-ground barrier.

CHAPTER 5

Trees, Shrubs, and Vines

TREES

SELECTION AND PLACEMENT

Diversity is important in an urban landscape. Before planting a tree, look around the neighborhood and see what other people are growing. Do not select those trees. Trees will be less likely to have problems in times of major disease or insect outbreaks if they are different species from the majority in the neighborhood.

Choose small to medium-size trees. Even a large city lot has room for only a few large trees. If it will have several trees, they should be small. Plan to put them where they will each have room to grow to their natural mature height and spread. Consider both overhead and underground utilities as well as buildings, sidewalks, driveways, and other paved or compacted areas. Tree roots do not grow well under paving or in compacted soil.

Be sure to put at least one deciduous tree to the southwest of the house and each outdoor living area that will be used in the summer. The shade the tree provides can make the area much more comfortable. To find the proper location for a tree, determine where the shade will fall in the summer. Find a long pole, a small branch that was pruned off another tree, or even a very large weed. On a sunny summer afternoon hold it up in

the air in different locations in the yard and observe where the shadows
fall. Mark planting locations where the shadow of the tree would shade
patios, parking areas, and windows of the house. This technique is reasonably accurate and fun. Be sure the tree is not too close to the house.
Most trees will be taller than the pole so their shade will stretch further.
You may also use a sun angle chart and find the proper locations for the
trees mathematically.

Many species of trees will do well in the Southwest. The table on pages
52–59 shows some of the characteristics of trees common to the Southwest. This list includes both desirable and undesirable trees. Examine
the characteristics before selecting a species. Some species, such as cottonwood and purple leaf plum, are combined because the characteristics
are similar. The height listed is an average height under cultivation. Many
of the trees will get larger in their native habitat; this should be kept in
mind if you are planting Ponderosa pine, Douglas fir, or other tall species
where they grow naturally. If the soil preference is listed as *tolerant* the
tree can survive in many soils; if it is listed as *adaptable* the tree will be
able to thrive in many soil types. A tree listed as a weed should not be

SMALL TREES

SCIENTIFIC NAME	COMMON NAME	HEIGHT	SPREAD	GROWTH RATE	ZONES	SOIL PREFERENCE[a]
Acer ginnala	Amur maple	15–18'	15–18'	Medium	2–7	Tolerant
Acer grandidentatum	Bigtooth maple	20–40'	40'	Medium	5–8	Tolerant
Aesculus californica	California buckeye	15–20'	10–15'	Medium	7–8	Dry alkaline
Albizia julibrissin	Mimosa	20–35'	20–35'	Fast	6–9	Adaptable
Cercis canadensis	Eastern redbud	20–30'	25–35'	Medium	4–9	Adaptable
Cercis occidentalis	Western redbud	10–12'	12–15'	Medium	7–9	Adaptable
Cercocarpuc ledifolius	Curlleaf mountain mahogany	15–30'	10–25'	Slow	3–8	Adaptable
Chilopsis linearis	Desert willow	15–35'	10–25'	Fast	7–10	Adaptable
Cotinus coggygria	Common smokebush	10–15'	10–15'	Medium	5–8	Adaptable
Crataegus crusgalli	Cockspur hawthorn	20–30'	20–35'	Slow–medium	3–7	Adaptable
Crataegus phaenopyrum	Washington hawthorn	25–30'	20–25'	Medium	3–8	Tolerant
Cupressus sempervirons	Italian cypress	20–30'	3–8'	Medium–fast	7–9	Tolerant
Elaeagnus angustifolia	Russian olive	12–30'	12–30'	Medium–fast	2–7	Adaptable
Forestiera neomexcana	New Mexico olive	8–25'	3–10'	Slow–medium	4–10	Adaptable
Juniperus monosperma	One-seeded juniper	10–20'	6–20'	Slow	4–9	Adaptable
Juniperus scopulorum	Rocky Mountain juniper	20–50'	10–30'	Medium	3–8	Adaptable

Note: Inclusion in this table does not indicate the tree is desirable. Examine characteristics before selecting species.

planted. Others with undesirable characteristics should be avoided in most situations but might be useful on a very difficult site.

Many new varieties of dwarf evergreens are available. Most of them prefer moist, cool areas. In a dry situation, piñon pine or some of the smaller junipers, which come in all sizes and shapes, would be more successful. For moister or easily watered situations, look for dwarf deodar cedar, dwarf spruces, mugho pine, and tanyosho pine. Every season brings new dwarf varieties to the nurseries. Be sure to find out the ultimate size of the variety before buying it. The newer varieties are quite interesting but may also be expensive because not many have been propagated.

Hundreds of different shrub junipers are available. They grow from four inches to twenty feet tall and spread from one foot to more than thirty. Form and size are the first considerations when shopping for a juniper. Next check whether it is male, female, or juvenile. A juvenile juniper will never produce mature type foliage or flowers. The foliage is awl shaped rather than scalelike. Female junipers produce berries. Female and juvenile shrubs will not produce pollen. Finally, check out color and the health of the particular shrub.

WIND DAMAGE	DISEASE	INSECT	POLLEN ALLERGY	POOR TRAITS	USE
Leafburn	Low	Low	—		Patio tree, screening
	Low	Low	—	Drops seeds	Fall color
	—	—	Assumed low	Drops flowers	Flowers, specimen
Breakage	High	High	Assumed low	Drops flowers, seeds	Flowers, light shade
	Medium	Low	Assumed low		Flowers, patio tree
	Low	Low	Assumed low		Flowers, patio tree
	Low	Low	—		Patio, specimen
Breakage	Low	Low	Rare	Drops seeds, flowers	Flowers, screen, specimen
	Low	Low	—		Color, accent
Leafburn	High	High	Rare	Thorns	Specimen, barrier, screen
	High	Medium	Rare	Thorns	Specimen, screen, barrier
	Medium	Low	High	Drops cones, scales	Formal arrangement
Breakage	High	Medium	Low	Drops fruit, leaves, twigs	Hedge, windbreak, small shade
	Low	Low	—		Patio, hedge, screen
	Low	Low	High (male)		Specimen, screen
	Low	Low	High (male)		Specimen, screen

[a]"Tolerant" means will survive in many soils; "adaptable" means will thrive in many soils.

SCIENTIFIC NAME	COMMON NAME	HEIGHT	SPREAD	GROWTH RATE	ZONES	SOIL PREFERENCE[a]
Maclura pomifera	Osage orange	20–40'	20–40'	Fast	4–9	Adaptable
Malus	Crabapple	8–40'	3–40'	Fast–medium	2–9	Adaptable
Pinus aristata	Bristlecone pine	8–20'	4–10'	Slow	4–7	Adaptable
Pinus edulis	Piñon pine	15–35'	10–35'	Slow	4–8	Adaptable
Poncirus trifoliata	Hardy orange	8–20'	6–14'	Slow–medium	6–9	Adaptable
Prunus cerasifera	Flowering (purpleleaf) plum	14–30'	15–25'	Fast	4–8	Adaptable
Quercus gambelii	Gambel oak	20–70'	15–30'	Slow	5–9	Adaptable
Quercus myrsinifolia	Chinese evergreen oak	20–30'	20–30'	Slow	7–9	Adaptable
Quercus turbinella	Shrub live oak	5–15'	3–15'	Slow	4–9	Adaptable
Rhamnus cathartica	Common buckthorn	18–25'	18–25'	Medium–fast	2–7	Adaptable
Robinia ambigua	Idaho locust	25–40'	15–30'	Medium	3–9	Adaptable
Robinia neomexicana	New Mexico locust	10–25'	8–15'	Fast	4–9	Adaptable
Salix matsudana (or hybrids)	Globe willow	20–40'	20–50'	Fast	5–8	Adaptable
Sambucus mexicana	Mexican elder	15–25'	15–25'	Medium	8–10	Adaptable
Tamarix ramosisima	Tamarisk (salt cedar)	10–15'	10–15'	Fast	2–8	Adaptable
Thuja orientalis	Oriental arborvitae	18–25'	10–15'	Slow–medium	6–9	Adaptable

MEDIUM TREES

Acer negundo	Boxelder	30–50'	30–50'	Fast	2–9	Tolerant
Acer planatnoides	Norway maple	40–50'	25–35'	Medium	3–7	Tolerant
Acer saccharinum	Silver maple	50–70'	30'	Very fast	3–9	Moist acid
Ailanthus altissima	Tree of heaven	40–60'	30–60'	Very fast	4–8	Adaptable
Calocedrus decurrens	California incensecedar	30–50'	8–10'	Slow–medium	5–8	Tolerant
Catalpa speciosa	Northern or western catalpa	40–60'	20–40'	Medium–fast	4–8	Adaptable
Cedrus deodara	Deodar cedar	40–70'	40–60'	Medium	7–8	Tolerant
Cedrus libani	Cedar of Lebanon	40–60'	30–50'	Slow	5–7	Tolerant
Celtis occidentalis	Common hackberry	40–60'	40–60'	Medium–fast	2–9	Adaptable
Cupressus arizonica	Arizona cypress	30–40'	15–20'	Medium	7–9	Adaptable
Fraxinus americana	White ash	45–60'	45–60'	Medium	3–9	Tolerant
Fraxinus oxycarpa "Raywood"	Raywood ash	40–50'	30'	Fast	5–8	Tolerant
Fraxinus pennsylvanica	Green ash	50–60'	30'	Fast	3–9	Tolerant
Ginkgo biloba	Ginkgo	50–80'	30–40'	Slow–medium	3–8	Tolerant
Gleditsia triacanthos var. inermis	Thornless common honeylocust	30–70'	30–70'	Fast	3–9	Adaptable
Juglans nigra	Black walnut	50–75'	50–75'	Slow	4–9	Tolerant
Juniperus virginiana	Eastern red cedar	40–60'	20–30'	Fast	3–10	Adaptable

Note: Inclusion in this table does not indicate the tree is desirable. Examine characteristics before selecting species.

WIND DAMAGE	DISEASE	INSECT	POLLEN ALLERGY	POOR TRAITS	USE
	Low	Low	High (male)	Drops fruit	Windbreak, rot–resistant wood
	High	High	Rare	Drops fruit	Flowers, fruit, fall color, patio tree
	Low	Low	Rare		Specimen
	Medium	High	Low		Specimen, screen
	Low	Low	Assumed low	Thorns	Barrier, screen
Leafburn	High	High	Rare	Poor structure, overused, short–lived	Specimen, grouping, foundation planting
	Low	Low	High		Shade, screen
	Low	Low	Medium		Patio or street tree
Leafburn	Low	Low	High		Patio, screen
	Low	Low	—	Thorns	Screen, hedge
	Low	Low	Low		Flowers, light shade
	Low	Low	—	Thorns	Barrier, flowers
Breakage	High	High	Low	Invasive roots, weak	Specimen, shade
	Low	Low	—		Specimen, patio, flowers
	High	Medium	Low	Weedy; crowds out native vegetation	Limited
Breakage, leafburn	Low	Medium	—	Overused	Specimen, hedge
Breakage	High	High	Medium	Drops twigs, seeds	Shade, screening
Leafburn	Medium	Medium	Rare		Shade, color
Breakage	High	High	Low	Drops twigs, seeds	Shade
Breakage	Medium	Low	Rare	Drops flowers, seeds, twigs; suckers, weed tree	Dry, harsh sites
Leafburn	Medium	Low	—		Specimen evergreen, screen
Some break-age	High	High	Low	Drops flowers, fruit	Shade, flowers
	Medium	Low	Rare		Specimen evergreen
	Low	Low	Rare		Specimen evergreen
	High	High	Low	Nipplegall on leaves	Shade, difficult situations
	Low	Low	High	Drops cones, scales	Specimen, screen, windbreak
	Low	Low	Medium		Shade, fall color
	Low	Medium	—		Shade, fall color
Breakage	Low	High	High	Drops seed; overused	Shade
Leafburn	Low	Low	Rare	Drops fruit, leaves	Specimen, fall color
Some break-age	High	Medium	—	Use thornless, seedless variety	Filtered shade
	Low	Low	—	Drops nuts	Shade, wood, nuts
	Low	Low	High (male)		Specimen, screen, hedge

[a]"Tolerant" means will survive in many soils; "adaptable" means will thrive in many soils.

SCIENTIFIC NAME	COMMON NAME	HEIGHT	SPREAD	GROWTH RATE	ZONES	SOIL PREFERENCE[a]
Koelreutaria paniculata	Goldenraintree	30–40'	30–40'	Medium–fast	4–9	Adaptable
Melia azedarach	Chinaberry	30–40'	30–40'	Fast	7–10	Adaptable
Morus alba	White mulberry	30–50'	30–50'	Fast	4–9	Adaptable
Morus rubra	Red mulberry	40–70'	40–50'	Fast	5–9	Adaptable
Paulonia tomentosa	Royal Paulonia	30–40'	30–40'	Fast	5–9	Tolerant
Pinus flexilis	Limber pine	30–50'	15–35'	Slow	4–7	Adaptable
Pinus nigra	Austrian pine	50–60'	20–40'	Medium	4–8	Adaptable
Pinus sylvestris	Scotch pine	30–60'	30–40'	Medium	2–8	Tolerant
Pistacia chinensis	Chinese pistache	30–35'	25–35'	Medium	6–9	Adaptable
Populus alba	White poplar	40–70'	40–70'	Fast	3–9	Adaptable
Populus tremuloides	Quaking aspen	40–50'	20–40'	Fast	1–6	Adaptable
Pseudotsuga menziesii	Douglas-fir	40–80'	12–20'	Medium	4–6	Tolerant
Pyrus calleryana	Callery (Bradford) pear	30–50'	20–35'	Fast	5–8	Adaptable
Quercus emoryi	Emory oak	30–60'	15–30'	Slow	6–9	Adaptable
Quercus muehlenbergii	Chinkapin oak	40–50'	50–60'	Medium	5–7	Rich alkaline
Quercus robur	English oak	40–60'	40–60'	Slow–medium	4–8	Tolerant
Quercus shumardii	Shumard oak	40–60'	40–60'	Slow	5–9	Tolerant
Robinia pseudoacacia	Black locust	30–50'	20–35'	Fast	3–9	Adaptable
Sallix alba "Tristis"	White willow (weeping)	50–70'	50–80'	Fast	2–9	Adaptable
Sophora japonica	Japanese pagodatree	35–75'	35–75'	Medium–fast	4–8	Tolerant
Thuja occidentalis	American arborvitae	40–60'	10–20'	Slow–medium	2–8	Adaptable
Ulmus parvifolia	Chinese (Lacebark) elm	40–50'	20–40'	Medium–fast	4–9	Adaptable
Ulmus pumila	Siberian elm	50–70'	35–50'	Fast	4–9	Adaptable
Zelkova japonica	Zelkova	50–80'	50–80'	Medium	5–8	Moist until estab- lished

LARGE TREES

SCIENTIFIC NAME	COMMON NAME	HEIGHT	SPREAD	GROWTH RATE	ZONES	SOIL PREFERENCE[a]
Carya illinoensis	Pecan	70–100'	40–75'	Medium	5–9	Tolerant
Gymnocladus dioicus	Kentucky coffeetree	60–75'	40–50'	Slow–medium	3–8	Adaptable
Metasequoia glyptostroboides	Dawn redwood	70–100'	25'	Fast	4–8	Moist, well drained
Picea pungens	Colorado (Blue) spruce	90–135'	20–40'	Slow–medium	2–7	Tolerant
Pinus eldarica	Afghan pine	70–100'	30–60'	Fast	7–10	Adaptable
Pinus ponderosa	Ponderosa pine	60–100'	25–30'	Medium	3–7	Adaptable
Platinus occidentalis	Sycamore	75–100'	65–80'	Medium	4–9	Tolerant
Platinus x acerifolium	London planetree	70–100'	65–80'	Medium	4–9	Tolerant
Populus nigra	Lombardy black poplar	70–90'	10–15'	Fast	3–9	Adaptable

Note: Inclusion in this table does not indicate the tree is desirable. Examine characteristics before selecting species.

WIND DAMAGE	DISEASE	INSECT	POLLEN ALLERGY	POOR TRAITS	USE
Some breakage	Low	High	—	Drops fruit, leaves, flowers	Flowers, patio tree
Breakage	Low	Low	—	Drops fruit; suckers	Shade in harsh areas
Breakage	High	Medium	High (male:	Drops leaves, fruit (female)	Shade
Breakage	High	Medium	High (male)	Drops leaves, fruit (female)	Shade, fruit
Breakage	Low	Low	—	Drops leaves, flowers, fruit	Shade, flowers
	Low	Low	Rare		Specimen
	Low	Low	Rare		Specimen
	Low	Medium	Rare		Specimen
	Low	Low	Rare		Shade
Breakage	High	High	High (male)	Drops leaves, fruit, flowers, twigs; suckers	Screen
Leafburn	High	High	High (male)	Weak, short–lived	Specimen, fall color
Breakage, leafburn	High	High	—		Specimen
Splitting	Low	Low	Rare	Poor structure	Specimen, flowers, fall color
	Low	Low	High		Shade. patio
	Low	Low	Medium		Shade
Leafburn	Low	Low	Medium		Shade
Leafburn	Low	Low	Medium		Shade, fall color
	Medium	High	Low		Flowers, light shade
Breakage	High	High	Low	Invasive roots	Specimen, shade
	Medium	Medium	—	Drops fruit, flowers	Shade, flowers, specimen
Breakage, leafburn	Medium	Medium	—	Overused	Specimen, hedge, windbreak
Breakage	Medium	Medium	High		Shade, specimen
Breakage	High	High	High	Weed tree	Limited
	Low	Low	—		Shade
	High	High	Medium	Drops fruit, husks, leaves	Nuts, shade
Breakage	Low	Low	—	Drops fruit	Shade
	Low	Low	—	Drops leaves	Specimen, screen
	Low	Medium	—		Evergreen
Some breakage	Low	High	Low		Specimen, screen
	Medium	High	Rare		Specimen, windbreak
Breakage	High	Medium	Medium	Drops leaves, twigs, fruit	Shade
Breakage	Medium	Low	Medium	Drops leaves, twigs, fruit	Shade
Breakage	High	High	High (male)	Weak, suckers	Screen

[a]"Tolerant" means will survive in many soils; "adaptable" means will thrive in many soils.

SCIENTIFIC NAME	COMMON NAME	HEIGHT	SPREAD	GROWTH RATE	ZONES	SOIL PREFERENCE[a]
Populus species and hybrids	Cottonwood	75–100'	50–75'	Fast	2–9	Adaptable
Quercus macrocarpa	Bur oak	70–80'	70–80'	Slow	2–8	Adaptable
Sequoia sempervirons	Redwood	60–300'	40–100'	Medium	7–9	Tolerant
Tilia americana	American linden	60–80'	30–60'	Medium	2–8	Adaptable
Tilia cordata	Littleleaf linden	60–70'	35–40'	Medium	3–7	Moist alkaline
Ulmus americana	American elm	60–80'	30–50'	Medium–fast	2–9	Tolerant
x Cupressocyparis leylandii	Leyland cypress	60–70'	12–15'	Fast	6–10	Adaptable

Note: Inclusion in this table does not indicate the tree is desirable. Examine characteristics before selecting species.

STARTING TREES FROM SEED

Many factors control whether the seed of trees will germinate. The seed must be collected at the right time, that is, after it is ripe but before it is too old. Many tree seeds remain viable for several years and some even have higher germination rates after a period of months or years than when they are fresh. An exception is acorns and fleshy seeds like magnolia that cannot be allowed to dry out at all. They should be planted as soon as they are collected, and only this year's crop should be collected. Other seeds should be dried and stored in a cool, dry place for short periods of time.

Some seeds, like piñon, have hard shells around them that should be scraped or nicked to allow the seed to absorb water and begin to germinate. This process is called scarifying and happens naturally either by physical damage as animals walk on the seeds, they are washed down creeks or blown around in windstorms, or when the seeds are eaten and scarred by the digestive fluids in an animal's stomach then passed through the digestive system. Scarification can be done artificially either by filing or sanding the seeds or by using sulfuric acid. Acid is dangerous, and filing is preferable for preparing a relatively small number of seeds.

Some seeds, such as stone fruit, need to go through a period of cold

WIND DAMAGE	DISEASE	INSECT	POLLEN ALLERGY	POOR TRAITS	USE
Breakage	High	High	High (male)	Weak; drops twigs, branches; suckers	Shade
	Medium	Medium	Medium	Drops acorns; large	Shade
	Low	Low	—	Too large for yard	Specimen
	Low	Low	Low		Shade, specimen
	Low	Low	Low		Shade
Breakage	High	High	High		Shade
	Low	Low	—		Screen, hedge

[a]"Tolerant" means will survive in many soils; "adaptable" means will thrive in many soils.

treatment after they are planted. Plant the seed outside in the fall so it will get a natural cold treatment in the winter and germinate in the spring.

Other seeds have substances in their seed coat that prevent germination. When rains have leached this substance out of the seed coat the seed will germinate. This insures that there is enough water to support the life of the plant when it does start growing. These seeds need to be soaked before planting. Many native desert plants use this mechanism to prevent germination at a time when they would not be able to survive.

Even with correct treatment tree seeds may take months to germinate. Once the seeds are planted, keep the seedbed moist until the plants germinate. Some seeds grow a small root in the fall and an aboveground sprout the next spring, so the germination process may be underway long before the first sign of life emerges from the soil.

Several references are available on seed germination. In *Southwestern Landscaping with Native Plants*, Judith Phillips talks about germination of native plants. An entertaining book on starting from seed is John Kelly's *Sowing a Better Garden*. This book was written in England and covers several plants that don't grow well here but it also gives a great deal of information on species we can grow. If instructions for sprouting a specific type of seed cannot be found in a reference, collect several of the seeds, divide them into lots, and treat each lot differently. Plant some seeds immediately and save others. Scarify some if they have a hard seed coat. Give some a cold treatment and plant some in warmer weather. Soak some and plant others without soaking. Try every combination of factors and keep good records. Most of all, be patient.

Many fruit trees are accidental hybrids that produce fertile seeds. The seed will sprout and produce a tree but that tree will have different characteristics from the parent plant and the fruit may not be as good. Since most trees do not produce fruit for several years, growing fruit trees from seed is a long-term experiment.

PLANTING

In mountainous areas and the northern part of the United States, tree transplanting should be done only in the spring. In other areas trees should be planted in the fall. They can establish roots while the soil is cool and days are short. Fall and winter, until the ground freezes, are the best times for root establishment. The trees will then be able to stand up to the wind in the spring, and the leaves won't dry out in the heat of the summer. The exception is stone fruit trees such as peaches or cherries. They should be planted in spring because they are not hardy enough to survive a hard winter.

Before planting a tree, locate underground utility access such as sewers and cable TV lines. Some trees, particularly poplar, willow, and tree of heaven, are notorious for clogging sewer lines. Check for overhead utility lines in the area before planting any tree that can be expected to reach more than twenty feet. Look around. A young spruce may be only three feet in diameter now, but when it reaches thirty feet, will the tree have to be mutilated to get cars into the driveway?

Directions for planting a tree depend on whether the soil is reasonably good or is caliche. If the yard is sandy or has good soil, dig a hole about twice the diameter but no deeper than the rootball or container. Remove the tree from the container, if it is containerized, and place it in the hole at the same level as it grew in the nursery. If the tree is balled and burlapped, place it in the hole as gently as possible. Dropping it could break the ball and destroy many of the roots. Be sure to remove the burlap or any other wrapping from around the sides of the rootball of trees and place it in the bottom of the hole. Trying to remove the wrapping completely may destroy the rootball. Cut away any wire around the rootball. Even wire with large spaces in it can cut into the roots as the tree grows. Backfill the hole halfway with soil. Do not add any fertilizer or amendments. Recent research has shown that improving the soil will encourage the roots of the tree to stay in the small improved area and not spread out, leaving few roots to support the tree. Fill the hole with water and let it soak in. Check the tree to see if it is still at the correct level, then finish backfilling the hole. Do not prune the tree. The buds at the tips of the branches produce a hormone that promotes root growth; pruning them off slows the establishment of the tree. Fertilize the tree with about half a pound of nitrogen in the spring.

In deep, solid caliche, tree planting is a different story. Dig a very large hole, almost like a pot for the tree to grow in. The tree roots will grow mostly in this hole, but they couldn't penetrate the caliche anyway, so by digging a big hole there is more soil than the tree would have otherwise. Try to dig a hole that is about five feet by five feet by five feet. Using a posthole digger or backhoe, or enlisting the assistance of bored teenagers, makes the digging much easier. If digging by hand, water the soil first, dig as far as possible then fill the hole with water again. When that water has soaked in (maybe a day or more) dig as far as possible again. Discard chunks of caliche. Mix the soil from the hole with well-rotted manure or compost and add some superphosphate or other phosphate fertilizer. Do not add any water soluble nitrogen. When this new, fertile soil is prepared, fill the hole with it and water it. Let it settle for a while so the tree does not sink into the soft soil when it is planted, then dig a small hole in the center and plant the tree as described above.

Regardless of the type of soil, be sure the hole is large enough to accommodate all the roots. The roots of a bare-root tree should be spread outward and downward, not stuffed into an undersized hole. When planting containerized trees, slip the tree out of the container, slice into the rootball with a sharp knife to cut any encircling roots, and cut off any roots that have reached the bottom of the container and begun growing in circles.

A tree that snaps off at the base without pulling up any roots probably had circling roots. If it was planted as a bare-root tree, the hole probably wasn't big enough and the roots were wrapped around the tree until they fit into the hole. If it was a container-grown tree, it was probably left in the container too long and the roots started growing around the edge of the container. The tree was then planted without cutting those roots, so they continued to grow in circles. As the roots and the trunk of the tree grew larger and larger, they grew together until the tree actually choked itself with its own roots. The roots restricted the growth of the trunk so much that it was not strong enough to hold up the tree in a windstorm, and it fell over. To check on other trees, dig down to the first roots and see if they are growing around the trunk. If the trees are still relatively young and only one or two roots seem to be growing in circles, cut those roots one at a time, allowing the tree to establish new roots before cutting any others. Cutting the roots is a repair job to correct a problem that should never have happened in the first place.

If someone else plants trees for you, make sure they plant the trees properly. Problems with encircling roots don't show up for several years, long after the original warranty has expired. Go to an established, rep-

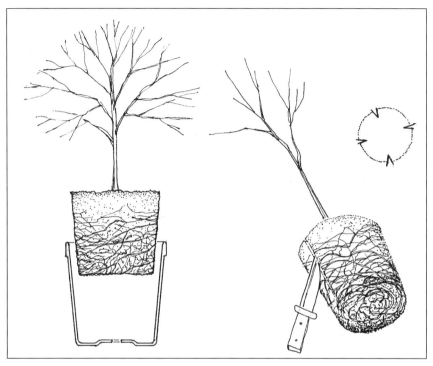

PLANTING A CONTAINERIZED TREE

utable firm. Check on their method of planting and the training of their work crews before hiring them.

A basin around the trunk is the best way to water a new tree. Water it every few days at first, then once a week through the first summer. In extremely hot weather water a little more frequently, especially if the soil is sandy. As the tree becomes established, the roots will start to grow outward and water will be needed outside the basin. After two years, level the basin and water the tree by laying a soaker hose in a spiral around the tree. Start about three feet from the trunk and end just outside the longest branches. Leave the water on until the water soaks into the top thirty inches of soil. The length of time will depend on the soil type. In

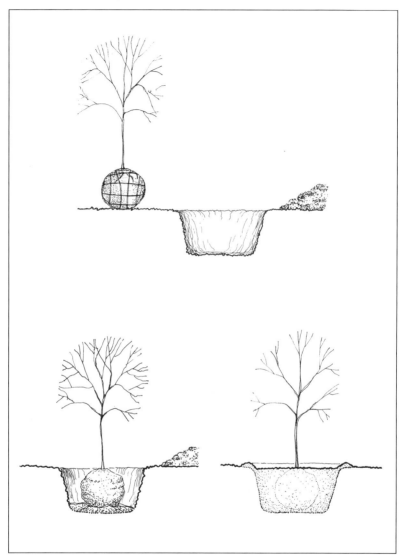

PLANTING A BALLED AND BURLAPPED TREE

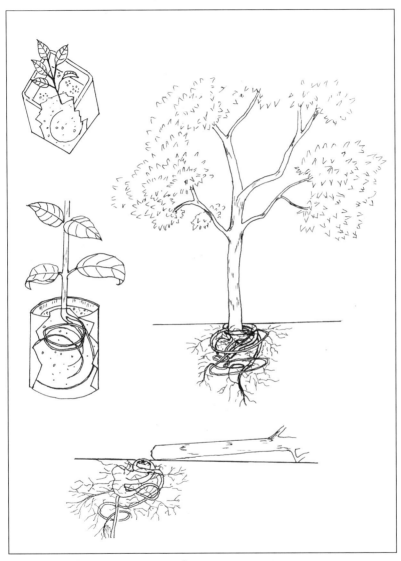

THE DEVELOPMENT OF CIRCLING ROOTS

very sandy soil during hot, windy weather, water in this way about once a week. In clay soil or if the temperature has been cool, once a month will be adequate.

A mature tree should be watered through the winter, every six weeks to two months, depending on the soil type, then watered at least once a month the rest of the year, making sure the water soaks in to a depth of two to three feet at each watering. Skip the August watering and go to the winter watering schedule in September to encourage the tree to go dormant early, which will reduce the chance of frost damage.

FERTILIZING

As a general rule, trees should not be fertilized unless they are growing very slowly or have yellowing leaves or needles. Young trees, however, will need moderate amounts of a complete fertilizer, especially if they are planted in poor, sandy soil. A complete fertilizer, known as NPK, is one that has nitrogen (N), phosphate (P), and potassium (K). In the Southwest it should also contain sulfur and iron. The relative amounts of those fertilizers are important, not the brand. The ratio of the three main elements is listed on the package as the analysis of the fertilizer. For trees, the best ratio is around 3:1:1. If a soil test has been done, follow the directions on the soil test report. They will be more accurate than these general recommendations. The proper ratio can be found in a fertilizer that has the numbers 30:10:10 or a fertilizer that has the numbers 9:3:3. If these two fertilizers were the same price per pound, the 30:10:10 fertilizer would be the better buy because it has more nutrients in it. Look for the most nutrients for the lowest price. A fertilizer that has lower numbers in the second and third positions (phosphate and potassium) will work too because those nutrients last for several years in the soil, whereas nitrogen leaches out very easily. Read the package carefully to find the amount of sulfur and iron. These are generally present in acidifying fertilizers. Iron and sulfur can also be applied separately, after the NPK fertilizer.

Trees should be fertilized only between the time they start growing in the spring and about the first of July. The amount of nitrogen determines the amount of fertilizer to apply. Apply up to 2 pounds actual nitrogen per year for every 1,000 square feet of area under the tree. A tree with 1,000 square feet would be 35 feet in diameter. A 2-year-old tree, for example, may cover an area of less than 100 square feet. To determine the area, find the diameter of the tree crown at the widest point. Divide the diameter by 2 to find the radius, then use the formula πr^2 to find the area. Divide this area by 1,000 then multiply by 2 to determine the number of pounds of nitrogen to apply. Then determine how much fertilizer will provide that much nitrogen. To do this, convert the first number on the fertilizer analysis from a percentage to a decimal (30 percent becomes .3, 8 percent becomes .08) and divide it into the amount of nitrogen needed. For example, if .1 pound of fertilizer is needed and the fertilizer has 30 percent nitrogen, use 1/3 pound fertilizer (.1/.3 = 1/3). Thus a tree less than 5 feet in diameter needs less than a pound of fertilizer per year.

Nitrogen should be applied in the spring when the leaves start growing so it can be utilized by the new leaves and twigs for growth. Most forms of nitrogen move easily through and out of the soil, so it should be applied only when needed to avoid polluting groundwater or surface runoff. Fertilizing trees with nitrogen in the fall produces a sudden spurt of growth that can easily freeze when the weather gets cold. Some trees, especially fruit trees that have produced heavily, could benefit from a fall application of phosphate fertilizers. Phosphates move through the soil slowly and although they are present in adequate quantities in many southwestern soils they are often present but unavailable in highly alkaline soils. They are essential to the growth of the plant, especially the roots and fruit.

One of the biggest problems with trees in the Southwest is iron deficiency. When a tree is deficient in iron, the veins are green but the leaves between the veins are pale yellow. Some of the leaves may even turn brown around the edges as if they are burned. In most cases, the soil has sufficient iron but the plants cannot pick it up because the soil is too alkaline. The problem can be solved either with foliar iron applications or by applying iron and acidifying materials to the soil. If a tree has a severe iron chlorosis problem, indicated by yellow leaves with green veins, plan on using a foliar spray in the spring just after the leaves come out and again in early summer. Follow the directions carefully; using too much iron spray on new leaves can burn them. Applying chelated iron to the soil will also help. Sulfur-containing fertilizers like iron sulfate and ammonium sulfate will make the soil less alkaline. Be sure to water the fertilizer in thoroughly after application so it is washed into the entire root zone.

One way to improve the soil over a period of time is to drill small holes about two feet deep just outside the drip line of the tree and fill the holes with one pound ammonium sulfate and one-fourth pound iron sulfate mixed with a five-gallon bucket of compost. Space the holes a couple of feet apart all around the tree. Do not use more than one pound of ammonium sulfate or five gallons of the mixture for every six inches in trunk diameter of the tree, and do this only in the spring and early summer. Mulch heavily with organic matter. If this is done annually the soil will become more acid over a period of years, and the tree will put out new roots into the improved area.

VALUE

Strong, healthy trees can be evaluated in several ways. If the tree was recently planted, the replacement cost would be the value of the tree. This replacement cost might be slightly different from the original cost of the tree because of changing prices.

A slightly older tree might be valued at the actual cost of caring for the tree plus compound interest on the investment. This formula includes original cost, land investment, and taxes on the land on which the tree sits; water, fertilizer, and pesticide costs; pruning costs and interest. Because some of the costs are difficult to determine and because interest rates have fluctuated so much over the past several years, this formula can get very complicated.

A more widely accepted formula is to calculate the cross-sectional area of the tree, multiply by a value per square inch, then multiply by percentage values based on the species, location, and condition of the tree. These things are best evaluated by a horticulturist or professional arborist. Call your county agent or a professional for assistance in applying the formula. If the tree is a mature, healthy specimen, this formula may be the best way to evaluate it. Otherwise, use replacement cost. A tree that was in poor condition and presented a hazard to people or property was a liability.

PRUNING

To determine what should be cut off a tree, as well as how and why it should be cut, you should clearly understand the principles behind pruning. Trees in a forest are never pruned; however, branches periodically die and fall off the tree. Foresters call broken branches hanging in a tree widow makers because they are so dangerous. When trees are in and around areas where people live and work, falling branches can be dangerous. The first reason for pruning is to keep people and their property safe. Remove dead or broken wood from a tree as soon as possible. Removing dead or damaged branches will not harm the tree and could save someone from injury. A professional arborist, who has the appropriate training and equipment, may be needed to remove a large branch. If many branches are dying, look for a potential root or trunk problem, which might require removing the entire tree before it falls.

Trees in the forest have an organic soil created by many layers of leaves falling to the ground and decomposing. The combined windbreak effect of all the surrounding trees helps protect each individual tree. Trees planted by people are almost always outside their natural ecosystems and so are under stress. Pruning should reduce stress rather than increase it. Practices that will increase the stress of a tree include cutting out more than one-third of the leaf area, leaving a stub of a branch, cutting into the wood of the trunk, and stripping the bark by failing to undercut large branches before removing them. All these practices are common among untrained tree pruners. Never allow trees to be topped, a practice that mutilates, weakens, and eventually kills trees. Trees that have been topped can be quite dangerous. According to one story, topping, or pollarding, started in Europe as a way to have a steady supply of firewood. However, cutting a large healthy branch off a tree weakens the tree and increases the chance of disease or insect attack. A tree that has outgrown its space can be reduced in size in ways that are less stressful to the tree and result in stronger new growth.

When pruning any woody plant, start by removing diseased branches. This will reduce the chance that the entire tree will succumb to the disease. Next cut out one of a pair of branches that rub against each other to reduce the chances of disease invading the tree. Thin branches in overgrown shade trees to reduce the chances of the tree being broken in a windstorm. Finally, prune for aesthetics. The basic growth pattern cannot be changed. A weeping tree cannot be created out of a purple plum. However the form can be shaped so it is more uniform or more informal. Training a tree to a specific shape should begin while the tree is still young. The Japanese go so far as to remove selected needles from pines. Americans generally prefer faster techniques, but branches should still be pruned selectively rather than lopped off indiscriminately.

Trees respond to pruning in different ways depending on their age and the time of year in which they are pruned. Pruning produces a flush of new growth. The heavier the pruning the more new growth there will be, and the faster the tree will grow. As a general rule the faster branches grow, the weaker they are, so severe pruning leads to fast, weak growth. Young trees will produce more new growth in response to pruning than more mature trees, although the ultimate effect of severe pruning will be to dwarf the tree because it has to put energy reserves into replacing the growth that was pruned off and has less energy for growing larger. Pruning in winter or early spring produces the most new growth. The energy reserves of the tree are still in storage, so when warm weather comes the tree is ready to put all its energy into growth. Pruning in spring just after the leaves have opened has the greatest dwarfing effect and pro-duces a great deal of stress. Energy reserves used to produce the new leaves have not yet been replenished by food produced by those leaves. Growth will be fast and very weak. Pruning in summer also has a significant dwarfing effect. By late summer and early fall, pruning should be avoided because the new growth that is produced will be more likely to freeze during the winter and the food reserves for the next year will be reduced. This is also the season when many fungi are sporulating, so disease is more likely.

If a young tree is properly trained as it matures little pruning will be needed when it is mature unless it is damaged or diseased. Do not prune the tree immediately after planting. A growth regulator produced in the tip buds of the plant stimulates root development; if those tip buds are removed the tree will take longer to become established.

After the tree has had a chance to establish itself, generally by the second winter, select the branches that will remain on the tree. If the tree has several branches coming from the same location, as it will if it was tip-pruned in the nursery, it will need extensive training. If the branches are desired at that level, select two to four branches that are evenly spread around the tree. Prune off other branches. The tree will fill in and be quite attractive without trying to strangle itself, which is what happens if all the branches are left on.

If people will be driving a vehicle or walking under the tree and the existing branches are not high enough, make the most vertical branch into a new leader. To do this, cut off the branches closest to the vertical branch so that it has room to grow. Cut back the other branches but do not remove them yet because removing that much of the leaf area would harm the tree. Later, when the tree is twenty to thirty feet tall, remove the lower side branches. By this time the new leader will have side branches at the appropriate height. Select the ones to keep and prune off the others. No more than a third of the leaf area should be removed at any one time. If one-third of the leafy growth is removed before a pruning job is complete, stop and wait until the next year.

If the tree was never tip-pruned in the nursery, simply select the branches you want to keep. To be able to walk under the tree, cut back side branches from the lower third of the trunk until the tree is more than twenty feet tall, then remove everything that is within eight feet of the ground. To drive under a tree, cut back the lower branches until the tree is thirty feet tall then remove anything within ten feet of the ground.

When the tree is five to ten years old, begin shaping the crown and perhaps thinning it to reduce wind resistance. To a certain extent this will depend on the natural growth habit of the tree. The goal is to have branches spaced far enough apart on the trunk so they can grow without interfering with each other. On a small ornamental tree the vertical spacing between branches could be as little as six inches, whereas on large shade trees it might be two feet. Select branches with a wide angle between the branch and the trunk. These branches coming from the trunk are called scaffold branches.

When the scaffold branches are established, start thinning side

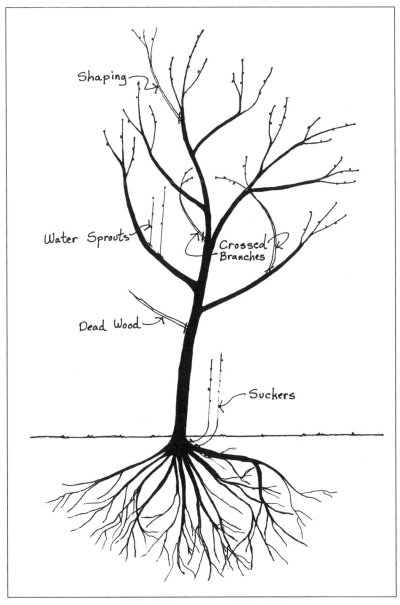

Shaping

Water Sprouts

Crossed Branches

Dead Wood

Suckers

PRUNING A TREE

branches along the scaffold branches if necessary. This process will be done in succeeding years, first along the lower scaffold branches, then moving up the tree.

Trees should have a single central trunk. If a tree has split branches near the top that appear to be equally dominant, remove one of them. Again, try to leave the one that will look best as the central trunk of the tree. This is generally the most upright one. If the tree is old and the two trunks are large, it is best to leave them.

If the tree was selected properly, the training process is complete when these side branches are selected and well spaced. Frequently, however, trees are selected with no knowledge of their mature height, and after several years the tree starts to outgrow the space in which it is planted. In such a case, talk to a reputable tree care firm about crown thinning or crown reduction, in which they will selectively cut up to one-third of the foliage branches of the tree. Selectively pruned trees grow back to their original height more slowly than topped trees, so in the long run it is not only safer but less expensive. Reducing irrigation and fertilization can also slow the growth of a tree, but this should be done carefully so the health of the tree is not jeopardized.

Any heavy pruning of evergreens is best done in winter because they are resting then. If the trees are pruned before Christmas the prunings can be used to decorate the house. The evergreens least affected by pruning are junipers and arborvitae, including the shrub forms and the trees frequently called cedars. Junipers and arborvitae can be sheared at any time of the year, or they can be cut back severely to reduce their size. To prune them, severely cut each branch back to a little wisp of green growth. If branches are cut off and stubs left, new growth may eventually sprout from the stubs or from the center of the plant but the plant will be unattractive for some time while this new growth develops. Cut the branch back to green growth and the small branchlet will soon hide the cut end.

Pines also tolerate pruning reasonably well, although new growth doesn't cover up mistakes as it would in denser evergreens. Plan cuts carefully when pruning pines and always cut back to a crotch or side branch. Cut ends of pine may exude large quantities of pitch if cut in late winter or spring. This is a natural way for the tree to protect itself and is nothing to worry about unless it drips on the sidewalk and gets tracked into the house. To reduce the problem, make pruning cuts in late fall or early winter, or even in summer on pines that come from cooler areas. Mountain pines in lower altitude areas will go dormant in the summer.

The ponderosa pine, as its name implies, is a very large tree in its natural habitat. Too often they are planted where a smaller pine would be more suitable. If a ponderosa or other large pine has been planted in an inappropriate location, cut the candles of new growth in half each spring, when it is easy to tell what is new and not too difficult to remove half of it. This will limit the amount of growth each year. Be sure to cut all the candles or there will be more growth on the uncut parts of the tree, which generally results in an unsightly shape. Do not remove the candles completely. Pine needles live only three years and if some new growth is not allowed each year the tree will soon be a mass of dying sticks with no needles to support them. Do not try this same method on a regular basis on spruce or fir trees.

Spruce and fir trees should not be pruned unless absolutely necessary. If they are infringing on sidewalks or driveways, branches should be removed at the trunk. If a spruce tree is growing unevenly the larger side can be reduced slightly by shearing, but if branches are cut off close to the center of the tree where there are no needles, new buds will not develop and the tree will always be poorly shaped. Fir trees do not react well to shearing or pruning. The Douglas fir is not a true fir and will grow new shoots to the side if it is pruned. If the top of the tree is cut out the tree will not grow taller, although occasionally a side branch of a young tree will begin to grow vertically and replace the leader.

Finding a reputable tree firm to do major work on trees is extremely important. The state of New Mexico does not have any professional licensing restrictions for firms involved in tree care, which means that some people who call themselves tree trimmers have no experience in tree care. A voluntary program to certify arborists was instituted in 1992, but not all reputable arborists have taken the certification exam. To select a company ask a favorite nursery or a landscape specialist for recommendations. Call each of the companies and ask the following questions.

What are the qualifications of the owners or estimators? What training do they have in tree care? What training is provided the crew that will do the job? Are they members of trade associations that help them keep abreast of the latest developments and newest treatments in tree care?

Does the firm give written price estimates? Ask for an explanation, preferably in writing, of exactly what needs to be done and why before you authorize any work. If you are not sure whether the work needs to be done, especially when considering the removal of a tree that is not dead, get a second estimate. If topping or severe pruning is recommended, be sure you understand why this decision was made. Such drastic work is seldom justified. Remember, a tree cannot be unpruned.

Will the trees be climbed using ropes or an aerial lift? Never hire a firm that uses climbing spikes to trim valuable trees. These spikes damage the living portion of the tree and open it up to infection. Spikes should be used only if a tree is to be removed.

Do employees comply with all safety standards? Will the work comply with all existing national standards for tree care? Ask about insurance coverage. Are all employees covered by workman's compensation in case of an accident? Is damage to your property covered? Are there any damage exclusions in the policy? Insurance is often a significant expense. An uninsured firm will be able to give you a lower estimate, but if any problems arise while work is being done on your property, you will have to pay the damages and may even become involved in a lawsuit.

Request a certificate of insurance if you are in doubt.

Can you get in touch with the company if there is a problem? A legitimate business can be reached if additional work is necessary and to help if a problem arises. Ask for references, then call to be sure they are customers. Drive by the site where the work was done. Do the trees look healthy?

The effort of finding a reputable tree care firm to take care of your trees is worth it when you consider that a mature tree can be worth several hundred or even thousands of dollars. A tree care professional should be concerned about the health, safety, and beauty of the

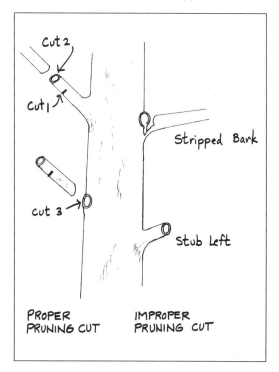

trees. Select a tree care firm carefully to preserve the value of the trees.

If you are going to be doing any pruning yourself, be sure tools are sharp and that you have the proper tools for the job. If a limb is too large to be removed with clippers or loppers, it should be removed with a saw using three cuts.. The first cut should be from the bottom of the limb upward, about twelve inches from the trunk or the larger branch from which the branch to be pruned is growing. The second cut should be from the top just a little farther out than the first cut. This will remove the branch but leave a stub. Do not leave that stub on the tree! Where the branch comes out of the tree will be a little bark collar. Cut the stub off at the edge of that collar. The collar is easier to see on some trees than others. Examine several trees before beginning to prune to determine where that collar is. Do not cut the stub off flush with the tree or healthy wood will be cut and the pruning wound enlarged.

Do not apply anything to the wound after the branch is cut off. The tree does not need any help in covering the wound, and some applications can actually slow the recovery process.

STRESS

Much of the Southwest is a natural grassland or desert. Trees are under constant stress simply because they are planted here. The soil and climate are not suited to the growth of trees except in the valleys and mountains, and even there we try to grow the woodland trees of the East rather than the native trees of the valleys and hills. The low level of organic matter and the high pH reduce the number of natural beneficial fungi in the soil and limit the availability of nutrients, while winds and long periods without rain dehydrate the leaves even when we irrigate. For this reason many tree species will be 15 to 20 percent shorter when they mature in the semiarid parts of the Southwest than they would in their native setting.

Often the things people do to trees cause them stress. A short-lived tree like cottonwood or Siberian elm can be expected to live 40 to 60 years under average conditions. A long-lived tree like an oak can live 300 years or more; 100 to 150 years is about average. Yet the average life span of an urban street tree is 7 years. Why do these trees, which we supposedly take good care of, die so soon?

The biggest reason is poor selection. Some trees, like maples, simply cannot grow well in our alkaline soils. Cottonwood and sycamore need to be able to reach the water table to be healthy, while piñon gets waterlogged and dies if its roots are wet all the time. A county extension agent, nursery professional, or various published plant lists can help select the tree that is right for a given situation.

Simply growing trees in an urban environment puts them under stress. Pollution, soil compaction, and construction damage are the most common causes of problems in urban trees. This stress can cause decline, which means the tree grows more slowly, is more susceptible to disease, and eventually dies.

Probably the number one cause of death among young urban trees is a condition known by tree care professionals as lawn mower blight. Young trees have thin bark, and directly under that bark is the only living, growing tissue of that tree trunk. If this green layer of tissue is destroyed, that part of the tree is dead. This tissue can be de-

---

Urban Tree Problems

"Lawnmower blight"—Caused by bumping a tree with equipment, cutting with a weed whip or rubbing by material used to stake the tree

Air pollution—American elm, catalpa. Lombardy poplar, Ponderosa pine, aspen and willow are particularly susceptible.

Chemical injury—salt used for melting ice, herbicides, etc.

Soil Compaction—foot or vehicle traffic or construction in the root zone of the tree.

Root injury—Trenching, change in soil level or construction around the tree.

---

stroyed by bumping it with a lawn mower or whipping it with a weed whip. Staking a tree with a garden hose that has wire run through it can also damage the growing tissue of the trunk. If this tissue is killed more than about halfway around any part of the trunk, the tree is likely to die. To protect the tree, mulch an area around it and pull any weeds that grow through the mulch so lawn equipment is never close enough to the tree to do any damage. Stake trees loosely and remove the stakes after the first year. Use a soft rubber tie like a section cut from an inner tube rather than a wire run through a garden hose.

Air pollution can also damage trees. The pollutants that cause the most problems for trees are ozone and peroxyacetyl nitrate. These pollutants come from auto exhaust and industrial emissions. Keep automobiles and other internal combustion engines tuned properly and follow burning ordinances. Trees that are particularly susceptible to air pollution injury are American elm, catalpa, Lombardy poplar, ponderosa pine, aspen, and willow.

Several other sources of chemicals can injure trees. Perhaps the most common are combination herbicide and fertilizer lawn products and deicing chemicals. Lawn fertilizers with weed killers in them should not be applied around trees. The broadleaf weed killers will be picked up by the tree roots. While there may not be enough of the chemical to kill the tree, it will weaken it and make it more susceptible to other problems.

Salt or calcium chloride is frequently used to melt ice on streets, sidewalks, and driveways. These materials are toxic to trees and can accumulate if they are used frequently. Use deicing compounds very carefully if any of the resulting slush could drain or be splashed under trees.

Soil compaction can be a problem in high-use areas such as around public buildings, near apartment complexes, and in parks. Compacted soil cuts off water and oxygen that are needed by the roots of the tree. Large roots near the base of the tree can also become exposed as the soil is compacted, creating a hazard for those who walk there and opening up the roots to injury. Walkways are sometimes designed too close to trees, but more often the problem is caused when people create a hard dirt path under a tree by using the area repeatedly as a shortcut.

Any disturbance of the ground under a tree can cause the gradual decline of the tree. Root injury is more likely to kill a tree than injury to the trunk, so be careful when doing any projects that require trenching near a tree. The addition of asphalt, concrete, bricks, or more than a few inches of soil under a tree can change the amount of water and oxygen available to the roots. Putting a small well around an established tree when soil is added or building a retaining wall under a tree within the drip line (the entire area under the branches) will not always pro-

tect it. If a tree is to be planted in a well, the well should be large, carefully constructed, and well planned.

The roots of a tree extend at least as far as the width or the height of
the tree, whichever is farther. In the case of many trees, cottonwoods
among them, the roots can extend much farther. Suckers or fast-growing sprouts can grow from these roots. Some trees naturally send up
suckers. Others sucker because they are under stress. First determine the
reason suckers are appearing. A tree of heaven or poplar tree will get
suckers no matter how it is cared for. A mulberry, linden, silver maple,
or crabapple is likely to get some suckers if it is healthy but will get many
more if the tree is stressed. Some other trees will send up suckers only as
a final attempt to survive. First examine the tree for injuries to the trunk,
such as from freeze injury or running into the tree with a lawn mower or
weed trimmer. Water stress can also produce suckers. If there is a severe
problem, it may be better to cut the tree down, letting one of the suckers become a replacement. A minor problem can frequently cure itself.
If the problem can't be located, cut the suckers off as close to the source
as possible. It may be necessary to dig down to a root to cut the sucker
off. Then water the tree thoroughly. Starting a few feet from the trunk,
spiral a soaking hose out to just past the edges of the branches and leave
it on very slowly all night. The water will soak far into the soil and encourage the roots to go deeper.

TREES IN LAWNS

Piñon trees and bluegrass are not compatible. Trying to keep a piñon
tree healthy in a bluegrass lawn is like trying to raise saltwater and freshwater fish in the same pond. However, some things can be done to keep
the piñon healthy. The biggest problems are with water and fertilizer.
Bluegrass needs lots of water and very fertile soil, whereas the piñon needs
less water and considerably less fertilizer. Water to a depth of at least
two feet once a month in the spring and summer. Leave the sprinklers

on longer than usual or spiral a soaker hose around the tree to a diameter of ten feet. This will water both the grass and the tree. Between deep waterings, leave the sprinklers on for a shorter period so the water only soaks into the first six inches of soil. Do not water deeply at all in August or September. This will keep the lawn growing while allowing the tree to go dormant. The bluegrass lawn will look best and be healthiest if it is fertilized in May, September, and November. The tree should not be fertilized after July. During the months of September and November, apply a slow-release fertilizer to the lawn, then water the lawn long enough to soak the fertilizer into the root zone of the grass but not deeper than six inches. Piñons grow slowly and do not need fertilizer if they have grown more than four inches at the ends of the branches within the last year. If the tree does need fertilizer, apply it in the spring. Find out how deep the roots of the grass go by digging a small hole in the grass with a shovel or soil probe. Place a slow-release fertilizer just below that point by pouring it into holes or slits made with a probe or shovel. Do not overfertilize.

Shade trees in lawns often have exposed surface roots that are damaged by lawn mowers and are a hazard to people walking on the lawn. Large roots cannot be cut off the tree without severely damaging the tree. The roots serve two purposes, to hold the tree up and to provide water and nutrients to the tree. The surface roots provide most of the nutrients and a great deal of support. If they are cut off, even on only one side of the tree, the tree is likely to fall over in the next big windstorm. If it does manage to remain standing, it will slowly starve until first one branch then another dies and must be pruned out.

The most common causes of surface roots are shallow or compacted soils, shallow watering, or high water tables. In a valley very close to a river, the water table may be high enough to cause roots to grow on the surface. In other areas the problem is more likely to be shallow watering or compacted soil. Existing surface roots cannot be forced to go deeper into the soil, but the tree can be watered more deeply if the soil is deep enough. If the soil is compacted use a deep tine aerator to loosen it. This will prevent more roots from growing at the surface. If the trees are growing in a shallow soil over rock not much can be done about surface roots. To reduce lawn mowing problems, plant an evergreen ground cover under the tree in the area where the surface roots are the largest. Ajuga or vinca would be good choices. Another solution is to remove the tree and dig out the roots, but most people prefer to remove a small area of lawn rather than a tree.

ROOT HEALTH

Remember that more than half a tree is underground. If an unhealthy tree has no apparent problem aboveground, look for root problems. Does the tree have black plastic under it? Has it been watered correctly? The soil should be moistened to a depth of thirty inches each time the tree is watered. This takes a lot of water. In a clay soil it takes more than in a sandy soil. After watering, let the soil dry out before you water again. A large cottonwood can use hundreds of gallons of water a day, whereas a piñon uses less water once it is established. As many problems are caused by watering piñons too frequently as by not watering them often enough. Are there rocks under the tree? If so remove the rocks from around the trunk and look at the lower trunk. When rocks are piled under trees, wind can cause the trunk to rub against the rocks. If the bark is damaged more than halfway around the tree, the tree may die. Keep rocks a few inches away from the trunks of trees so the rocks do not kill the tree.

If the roots of trees or shrubs are covered with plastic or paving, the plants will start to decline over time. The plastic will cut off the supply of water and oxygen to their roots. Large, established plants will be more affected than young plants, although damage will not show up for some time. The roots of woody plants continue to grow outward each year. The part of the root that absorbs water and nutrients is close to the growing tip of the root. If the surrounding soil is well watered and aerated, the roots grow into the soil, absorb plenty of water and nutrients, and can support strong, healthy growth on the leafy portion of the plant. If the soil is not well aerated or moist, the roots are stunted; therefore the upper portion of the plant is stunted. Under heavy plastic, lack of oxygen is the bigger problem. Water can flow under the plastic, but oxygen is excluded. The roots of the plant grow along the surface of the soil in an attempt to absorb moisture and oxygen. This shallow, poorly developed root system reduces the plant's resistance to environmental stresses, insects, or disease. Keep plants healthy by puncturing the plastic a number of times around the trees. The holes should be placed within an area about three feet either side of a line directly under the tips of the branches. This will not have a significant effect on the number of weeds that come up through the rocks. Most weed seeds need light to germinate, and it will still be dark under the rocks. Puncturing the plastic will provide enough water and oxygen to help the plants survive several years longer than they would with the plastic covering their root system. A better solution is to use a woven weed barrier rather than plastic under rock mulch.

INSECTS AND DISEASE

Heavy infestations of piñon needle scale can kill young evergreen trees and make larger trees more susceptible to invasion by bark beetles or other insects. The heaviest infestations generally come in late spring, but warm weather may cause the females to emerge earlier. Look for clusters of yellow eggs held together by cottony webbing and destroy these egg masses. Once the scale insects emerge from the eggs they crawl up the trunk of the tree and insert their mouth parts into the needles. They then coat themselves in a waxy covering and are very difficult to eliminate. If the crawler stage is present on the tree, spray with an insecticide recommended for pine needle scale.

Clusters of white bumps are pine needle scale. They hatch out in the late spring. The small insects crawl to the new needles of pines and spruce, pierce them, then suck sap from the plant. Their bodies develop a white crusty shell. The females will lay eggs from which will hatch a second generation of insects in midsummer. They can be controlled by a systemic insecticide. Be sure scale is listed among the pests it kills and pine and spruce are listed among the plants it can be used on.

Almost every type of tree can get borers. Wood borers are generally the larvae of beetles or moths, and with a few exceptions they attack only trees have been weakened by stress. Periodically there seem to be an unusually large population of borers. Borers are difficult to control because they are deep inside the tree, frequently in areas that contain many dead cells, so even a systemic pesticide will not kill them. The adults emerge, mate, and lay eggs. If the eggs are not laid inside the tree by the female adult, the larvae burrow back into the trees when they hatch out. The best time to control borers is when either the adults or the larvae are outside the tree. This is a different time for each species. Some of the factors predisposing trees to borer attack include underwatering; freeze injury; injury resulting from overpruning or topping; defoliation by leaf-eating insects, or construction activities; or chemical injuries. Freeze injury and physical injury from weed whips and lawn mowers are the most common cause of borer susceptibility.

To control borers, first identify the species, find out about its life cycle, determine how much damage it is capable of doing, then use an effective control measure at the right time. Your county extension agent can help identify the type of insect and tell you about its life cycle. You may want to hire a professional pest control applicator with training in integrated pest management. The applicator would have to identify the species of borer and scout the area for adults in order to know when to spray.

Borer crystals repel moths and kill their larvae. They are made of paradichlorobenzene, one of the chemicals used to make moth crystals. To be effective they must be used against borers whose adult form is a moth that attacks the tree near the base of the trunk. Borer crystals are most effective against peach tree borers and should be used around the base of stone fruit trees each fall. Only one company, Fertiloam, still produces borer crystals.

A likely cause of cottonwood problems in midsummer is borers. At least five different species of beetle larvae feed on cottonwood trees, but the most damaging is the longhorn beetle. These are very large beetles, up to one and a half inches long, with black bodies covered with tiny white hairs, which makes them look gray from a distance. The larvae bore into the tree and spend two years feeding on the tree before they emerge as adults. The adults mate and lay their eggs at the base of the tree, then new larvae hatch and bore into the tree again. The beetles begin appearing in large numbers in mid- to late summer. The longhorn beetle can be controlled effectively only by spraying the adults before they lay their eggs. Watch for them to emerge each July and use a pesticide labeled for the beetles when they first appear.

Borers in ash trees could be any one of three pests: flatheaded apple tree borers, lilac or ash borers, or banded ash clearwings. The damage in each case is done by the larvae of a beetle or moth that eats its way through the wood, pupates inside the tree, then emerges as an adult to lay eggs and start the process over again. Flatheaded apple tree borer larvae may even enter and enlarge the same tunnels created by their parents the previous year. Flatheaded apple tree borers and lilac or ash borers emerge from the tree in the spring; the banded ash clearwing emerges in August.

The apple tree borer can be identified by an oval or D-shape exit hole and by frothy sap emerging from the hole and from cracks in the bark. Generally, frass, or sawdustlike material, will be in the hole. The presence of flatheaded apple tree borers is generally an indication that the tree was stressed in some way, often by high summer temperatures or damaged bark. Cut out the dead branches and water well, particularly through the summer. To control a sever infestation, treat the trunk in

May with pesticides labeled for borers. Fertilize the tree in the spring to encourage growth. Also examine the growing area of the tree to see if the roots could have grown into an area of poor soils or an area where herbicide had been applied.

Lilac or ash borers characteristically keep their tunnel clear from debris, and the exit hole is a sunken, round hole. Sawdust will collect on the ground or in the sap around the hole. Lilac or ash borers are the most common borers on ash trees in this area. Pupal cases of the lilac borer, but not the banded ash clearwing, can be found on the trunk or branches just after the borers emerge. The banded ash clearwing looks and acts similar to the lilac borer but emerges in late summer rather than spring. Pheromone traps are available to determine when the adults are present and thus when the tree should be treated. Pesticides labeled for borers can be used on the lilac borer; use Dursban on the banded ash clearwing.

If a pine is dropping needles or they are turning yellow, first examine the trunk and root area for possible problems. If both the trunk and the roots are healthy, start up the trunk looking for broken limbs, bark damage, or borer holes. Most evergreen borers attack trees that are already weakened in some way, such as by over- or underwatering, herbicide damage, or other stress. Borers can be treated with insecticides, although only a couple of products are still on the market.

Larvae or caterpillars of the pine tip moth bore into the tips of branches and cut off the water and nutrients, so the tips beyond the point where the caterpillar entered turn brown. Pine tip moths have been monitored in several areas of New Mexico for several years through the Cooperative Extension Service Integrated Pest Management program. Monitoring moth flights determines when the population of the larvae will be at its peak and therefore when control measures will be most effective. After emerging and mating, the moths lay their eggs on the pine trees. The use of sprays as these eggs hatch, one to two weeks after the peak flight, gives the most effective control. The pine tip moth population can have three peaks and require three sprays a year, although two are more common in the Southwest.

Pine trees, especially piñon, lose pitch rather than the thinner less sticky sap of deciduous trees. The most common cause of "bleeding" piñons is the pitch moth. The larvae of the pitch moth bore into the tree and start the pitch flowing. They then feed on this pitch. The result is great masses of frothy pitch on the trunks or branches of young piñons. Other borers can also cause similar problems although the pitch flows are generally smaller and less frothy.

Red spider mites are quite common on evergreens during hot, dry periods. The tiny red mites are not really spiders, but are more closely related to spiders than to insects. A heavy infestation will whiten the needles and dark webbed masses will begin to show up in the center of the plant. A very heavy infestation can kill the most affected branches. Shake one of the affected branches over a white piece of paper. Tiny red specks scurrying around on the paper are the mites. The easiest way to control them is to spray the evergreens regularly with water. Red spider mites like dry, dusty places and after they are washed out every day for a week or two, they will disappear.

"Pine cones," or brown prickly growths, at the end of spruce branches are a gall caused by an insect called an adelglid. Similar to an aphid, it spends half its life in the galls on spruce trees and the other half on Douglas fir. The egg masses are white cottony tufts. Insects will emerge from the eggs in early summer. They will inject a toxin into the twigs just below the bud and new galls will form. When they are active they can be controlled by Carbaryl but later the galls will have to be cut off to control the insects. Spray once when the eggs are hatching and once in about a week. Licensed applicators can use stronger, more effective chemicals.

Euonymous scale is quite common on euonymous shrubs, and somewhat difficult to control. While the weather is still cool, an oil spray can be used, perhaps in combination with an insecticide. Be sure to buy an

oil spray that can be used on broadleaf evergreens and follow the directions for diluting it. If the mixture is too strong, it can damage the euonymous. Do not spray when night temperatures are expected to go below
freezing or when daytime temperatures are expected to exceed eighty
degrees. If the problem persists after the proper use of the oil spray, try a
systemic insecticide. Look for one in which the active ingredient is
acephate. Read the label carefully to make sure it can be used on broadleaf evergreens. If the infestation is too severe, the plant may need to be
cut to the ground and new growth sprayed in June with the pesticide containing acephate.

Two types of worms are commonly found on yucca. One is the larvae
of a moth. They bore into the base of the leaves and are relatively harmless. The other is the larvae of the agave weevil, which probably kill more
yuccas than any other insect and may be second only to overwatering as
the cause of death of the larger yuccas. The larva looks like a white grub
without legs. It bores into the center of the plant, seeking the tender growing tip in the heart of the plant. Plants infested by the weevils are likely
to be attacked by bacteria and break down into a smelly mass of tissue
and woody fibers. Pupae in cocoons made of the woody fiber are likely
to be in this bacterial mass. Infested plants should be completely removed,
including the underground parts of the crown because they probably hold
pupae for the next generation. To control the insects with pesticide, a
chemical labeled for weevils must be applied when the adult weevil is
present. The adult is a large, long-nosed black beetle. The body and snout
shape resemble the common flour weevil, but it is closer to a large cock-
roach in size.

While many fungi require humid weather to thrive, powdery mildew
is less particular. It can attack certain susceptible plants like grapes, lilacs,
roses, and zinnias in just about any weather. A heavy infection will pro-
hibit the leaves from manufacturing food for the plant, and the plant
will be weakened. The infection can frequently be reduced by thinning

the growth to improve air circulation around the remaining leaves. To control the infection, spray the top and bottom of the leaves with a fungicide labeled for use on the affected plant. Repeat the treatment every seven to ten days until the fungus is under control. Misuse of some of the fungicides can burn the leaves and cause them to fall off.

Brown horned growths on cedars are caused by cedar apple rust, a disease that spends part of its life cycle on cedar trees and part on apple trees. The little spikes will grow into gelatinous orange horns. It looks rather frightening but is not much of a problem on cedars.

The disease is more of a problem on apple trees. It causes spots on leaves and fruit, and the fruit can drop off early in infected plants. The growth on cedar trees releases spores that will infect any apple trees within several hundred yards. Prune out the infected cedar branches, and if apples are grown nearby, spray them with a fungicide containing zinab or ferbam when the buds show color, again when 75 percent of the petals have fallen, and once more ten days later.

One of the most common diseases of fast-growing trees is a bacterial disease called slime flux that causes a whitish or yellowish fluid to come out of the tree. Slime flux alone seldom kills trees, but it can weaken them enough that other stresses kill them. A tree with slime flux will live longer if it is fertilized each spring and watered well all year long. Slime flux enters through wounds. These wounds are most often pruning cuts, other mechanical wounds, or bark cracks caused by freezing.

Poplars, cottonwoods, and other fast-growing trees are susceptible to several fungi. Black spots on the twigs could be cytospora. A systemic fungicide can help control the fungus, but it generally attacks only trees that have been weakened by other problems. Try to determine and correct watering or other maintenance problems before resorting to a fungicide. By the time cytospora infects a tree, it is often too late to save it.

Pine needles naturally turn brown and fall off the tree when they are a few years old. If the needles that are turning brown are toward the center of the tree and the newer needles at the ends of the branches are still green, there is nothing to worry about. However, if the tips of new needles turn brown, the tree may not have received enough water in the summer.

If the tree was watered well all summer and the new pine needles have definite spots on them or rings around them, the problem could be a fungus. Several fungi affect pine trees, and effective control depends on proper identification. Diseased needles can be brought to the County Extension Office for diagnosis and recommended treatment.

WINTER INJURY

Temperatures between freezing and about 55°F help prepare trees for winter. Cooler temperatures, along with shorter days, signal the tree that it is time to go dormant. When we have some early cool nights rather than a sudden drop to below freezing, we should have a wonderful fall and limited winter damage to trees.

A sudden drop in temperature can cause tree problems. If this occurs in the fall or spring when the tree is not dormant, the leaves, buds, and sometimes the twigs will freeze and die, which weakens the tree. If the sudden temperature drop is severe enough, the live wood will actually freeze and split, killing the tree immediately. A more common problem is minor damage to the live portion of the tree, which kills a portion of the tree. If the problem is severe enough, the tree will slowly decline over the next several years, losing a few branches at a time. Either the entire tree or a section of the tree will die as much as ten years later.

Temperatures below minus 10°F will damage some trees and shrubs that are normally hardy in this area. Buds may be frozen, or on particularly tender plants, whole branches may die back. Evergreens may begin to look pale and dry. Plants covered with snow are somewhat protected. Exposed plants are the most likely to be damaged. Damage will not be evident until spring. If the buds were frozen, new leaves will not appear at the normal time. The trees and shrubs will develop new buds but may not leaf out until almost summer. If branches have been frozen, they may not leaf out at all or they may leaf out then drop their leaves when the weather gets hot. If this happens, wait until summer then prune out anything that is dead.

Desiccation of evergreens is drying of the plant. In the Southwest, this happens in winter when cold, dry winds hit the tree or in summer on newly planted evergreens. Generally it will be worst on the outside of the plant on the side facing the strongest wind or brightest sun. Desiccation causes the plants to turn gray or whitish. Depending on how quickly the desiccation occurred, the plants can be faded green to pure white. Needles and branch tips will be brittle, with larger twigs underneath remaining supple. These twigs are still alive and will produce new growth. Only occasionally is desiccation so bad it will kill large sections of the tree. If evergreens are dry and brittle for no apparent reason, it is probably the result of winter desiccation.

Preventing winter desiccation of evergreens is a year-round process. During the spring and summer water sufficiently for good growth but do not overwater the trees. Water well out from the trunk to encourage the development of an extensive root system. In pure sand, frequent watering is necessary, but watering every day is not, particularly in late summer and fall. Cut back on water in fall to begin to harden the trees off. By the time the first winter winds come, the trees should not have any pale green new growth. It should all be the deeper green of mature growth. Do not give the trees any nitrogen fertilizer at this time, although some phosphorous might be beneficial if a complete fertilizer has not been used.

During the winter, water once a month under the tree and in an area about twice the diameter of the branches to provide a reservoir of water for the roots to extend into. The roots will keep growing into moist soil as long as it is not frozen.

Antidesiccants should be used only on newly transplanted evergreens or on evergreens that have a great deal of tender new growth when winter comes. An antidesiccant is an oil or wax that coats the leaves and does not let water evaporate from them. Not just any oil can be used. Some oils act as herbicides. Use a product labeled as an antidesiccant if necessary.

When the wind blows hard, as it often does in the spring, it dries out all living things and sandblasts new leaves. If a tree has been dehydrated by spring wind, give it plenty of extra water. Use a soaker hose or other slow application system to apply water all the way around the tree starting a few feet from the trunk and going outward to just beyond the tips of the longest branches. Leave the water on until it has soaked deep into the soil. If the twigs and buds are not desiccated, the tree will start to grow again.

This would be a good time to leach the salts in the soil below the root zone. To do that, water long enough to let the water soak into the soil about four feet. In some soils this will take a couple of days and the water will have to be applied very slowly. In other soils it can be accomplished more quickly.

CLIMATE AND WEATHER

The Southwest has several ecosystems, or life zones, that are determined primarily by altitude and defined by the trees that live there. To learn about the primary species in several life zones drive up the road to Sandia Peak, reading the signs along the way. Generally, a plant can be brought down one life zone without any problem. A ponderosa pine will do well in the piñon-juniper belt that makes up the higher altitude areas of Albuquerque. Moving a plant down two life zones, such as moving the ponderosa pine to the desert area of Socorro or moving an aspen to the piñon-juniper belt puts the plant under climatic stress. Moving a tree down three life zones, such as bringing the alpine fir to Albuquerque, causes extreme stress to the tree, and it can survive only in the most carefully created microclimate. It will have the best chance of survival if planted on the north or east side of the house. Water it more than other trees in the yard, and mulch the soil under and around the tree with a thick layer of organic mulch to keep the soil cool.

POLLEN ALLERGIES

Pollen allergies are quite common in Albuquerque because of the pre-dominance of male, wind-pollinated plants. Some years pollen counts are higher than other years. A variety of things can cause high pollen counts, including low pollen production the previous year, stress the previous summer, good water supplies in fall and winter, and perfect weather for pollen production in spring.

Windblown pollen is the culprit in most pollen allergies. Most flowers and vegetables are insect pollinated, but many trees, weeds, and grasses are wind pollinated. They produce large quantities of pollen that is then blown around in the wind until it sticks to something. During the time that most of Albuquerque's residential areas were being developed, male trees were specifically planted. Males do not produce fruit, so there is no cotton flying around in summer from the cottonwood trees and no mulberries falling from mulberry trees to stain everything in sight. But there is a lot of pollen in the spring. When the wind is particularly strong and persistent, it keeps the pollen in the air and blows dust around, which can also contribute to sinus problems.

In an effort to reduce pollen allergy problems, some trees have been banned in Albuquerque. Planting mulberries, nonnative cottonwoods, elms, male junipers over five feet tall, or cypress is now illegal.

PIÑON NUTS

Piñon trees have male and female flowers on the same plant. Every piñon tree can produce nuts, but it must be pollinated by another tree. A tree might not produce nuts for several reasons. One reason is that the tree is young and is not producing cones yet. Once the tree starts to produce flowers, it takes three years for the tree to produce mature seeds. During that time a number of things can happen to prevent seed production. If a heavy frost occurs while the pollen is being formed, the pollen can be sterile. Later, when the female cones are being produced, a sudden cold snap can freeze them and make them invible. Spring rains can prevent the pollen from being released from the male cones. Piñons are wind pollinated, and lack of wind or prolonged strong winds can reduce the rate of pollination. Once the female cone is pollinated, insects can eat the seeds out of the cones, or rodents can steal the seeds just before they mature.

> ## Common Pollen Sources
> ### Trees
>
> (only males produce pollen but females often produce nuisance seeds)
>
> green ash
>
> osage orange
>
> mulberries
>
> cottonwoods
>
> Siberian elm
> (Lacebark elm is a less serious problem)
>
> junipers
>
> cypress.

Once the cones are mature there will usually be two kinds of seeds in them. Light tan ones do not contain any nuts; darker ones are more likely to. The light tan ones were pollinated with pollen from the same tree. The closer the tree is to another piñon tree the more likely it will have a good crop of nuts. If no other piñon is within a mile of the tree, it is unlikely to produce many nuts. After producing a particularly heavy nut crop, the tree is not likely to produce another heavy crop for at least two or three more years.

SHRUBS

Fall is the best time to plant shrubs. Even though the top portion of the plant is going dormant, the roots continue to grow until the soil is frozen. Roots of shrubs planted in October will continue to grow until about

December, and the shrubs will be able to start growing sooner and survive drought better next spring. To become well established, shrubs should have at least a couple of months of root growth in cool but not frozen soil before the leaves come out. In the warmer parts of the region the shrubs can be transplanted in winter.

Some species of shrubs are hardier and can tolerate late transplanting better than others. If the shrub is tender, do not transplant it until spring. One way to tell if it is tender is to find out if it can be grown a hundred miles north or a thousand feet higher than where you live. If the shrub cannot survive in those colder areas of the region, do not transplant it in the fall.

Weekly watering is adequate for newly planted shrubs if they get enough water each time. Soak the soil thoroughly with each watering to the same depth as the hole that was dug when the shrubs were planted. In a heavy soil, cut back on the frequency of watering in late summer. The next year water a little farther away from the base of the shrub and water for the same length of time each watering. Reduce the frequency to once every two weeks.

If foundation shrubs have grown too tall and are hiding the windows, the best thing to do with those shrubs is to transplant them to a part of the yard where they have enough space and put something else under the window. First decide where to plant them. Make sure the area is large enough for the mature size of the shrubs. Dig a hole in the selected site for each shrub. The hole should be at least twenty inches deep and as wide as the shrub that will be planted there. To transplant the overgrown shrubs, dig a trench around the entire shrub. Leave as much of the root system as possible. Dig down twenty to thirty inches, then carefully cut the roots under the ball of soil. Have a big piece of burlap or canvas ready. Roll one end of the cloth, tip the root ball, and put the roll under the rootball. Tip the plant the other way and unroll the cloth so the shrub is sitting on the piece of cloth. Two people can then carry the shrub to the new location. Lower it into the hole, remove the cloth carefully, then fill in the soil around the roots and water it well. Make sure the shrubs are not planted any deeper than they were growing in the previous location.

> ## Common Pollen Sources
>
> ### Shrubs
>
> sagebrush (Artemesia tridentata)
>
> four-wing saltbush
>
> male junipers

After transplanting the shrubs, some soil will be left over. Use that to fill in the holes under the window, then plant low-growing plants there. Use something like creeping sumac or cushion mums if it is on the west side, creeping mahonia or ivy on the north or east side, or lavender cotton, snow-in-summer, or desert zinnia on the south.

When planting containerized shrubs be sure to remove them from the container and slice through the sides of the root ball to encourage roots to grow out into the soil. Fertilizing or amending the soil is not necessary, although it is advisable to loosen the soil around the planting area by digging or tilling if possible. Water the shrubs as soon as they are planted and keep them well watered until they are established. Water so that the top eighteen to twenty-four inches of the soil is moist. Mulch will help control weeds around the shrubs and conserve water.

Most shrubs should be pruned annually. Some shrubs can be cut all the way back to the ground and come back. These include lilacs, flowering quince, and pyracantha. Other shrubs, like boxwood or magnolia, should not be pruned so severely. There are two basic pruning techniques for shrubs. One is to cut entire branches out at the ground. This is the technique to use if the shrub is too thick and has too many branches from the ground. The other technique is to cut back each branch. Start a pruning job by pruning out anything that is dead or dying. Next, remove diseased wood. After each cut on diseased wood, dip tools into a 10 percent chlorine bleach solution. If any of the branches are crossed and rubbing against each other, cut one of the crossed branches off.

The next step is to decide if the shrub is to be open centered or upright. This depends on the natural growth habit of the shrub and how disease resistant it is. If it is prone to fungal diseases like powdery mildew, an open center is generally better. Some plants have such upright growth habits it is difficult to get them to grow with an open center. When the desired shape of the shrub is determined, remove up to one-third of the remaining branches, either from the inside for open centered shrubs or from the entire shrub for upright shrubs. Step back and look at the shrub after each cut to make sure the shape is attractive and to determine where to make the next cut. Try to avoid cutting too much off. Finally, cut back any branches that are growing too vigorously. Do not cut into the older wood on these branches, just remove some of the newer growth.

Spring-flowering shrubs should be pruned after they flower. If they are pruned in fall, winter, or early spring all the flower buds will be cut off. Late summer– and fall-flowering shrubs or shrubs grown for foliage, shape, or reasons other than flowers should be pruned in winter.

One of the most important factors in pruning hedges is to allow it to grow slightly larger each year. Rather than cutting the hedge to the same height each year allow about one-half inch of new growth. This will make the hedge greener and more attractive. The new growth will produce food for the plant and keep it healthier. If all the new growth is removed, the hedge is more susceptible to sunscald, disease, and winter injury. Fertilize evergreen hedges after spring pruning to help them recover from the shock. Apply a 10 percent nitrogen fertilizer at the rate of one cup per four feet of hedge.

A fan-shaped hedge is a problem. The bottom leaves get shaded out by the upper ones. A sheared hedge should always be wider at the bot-

CUTTING BACK AN OVERGROWN SHRUB

tom than the top so the bottom leaves can get some sunshine. If the plants
in the hedge are very large, with heavy trunks, it may be better to start
over to get an attractive hedge. Many of the plants used in hedges are
extremely resilient. They can be cut down completely then come back
even thicker. It might be best to cut the hedge down and shear it to a
more appropriate shape when it grows again. Do not try this with boxwood hedges, however.

   If the hedge is necessary for privacy or traffic control, try to renovate
it more gradually. Cut the hedge lower than normal. This will encourage growth farther down the plants. Then gradually reverse the shape so
that the narrowest part is at the top. Wait until there is some growth at

PRUNING AN UPRIGHT SHRUB

the bottom, then allow this growth to become as wide as the hedge will be before shearing it. While the bottom is growing out, continue to shear the top, making it gradually narrower. The hedge will remain healthier and more attractive as it is growing out if not more than one-third of the leafy growth is removed at any one time.

Pyracantha is one of the most commonly used broadleaf evergreens for hedges in the Southwest. Once established, pyracantha is relatively drought tolerant and needs little fertilizer, but it is a very poor choice for a narrow space. Pyracantha shrubs tend to spread several feet in all directions. They grow rapidly when conditions are right and unless they are pruned frequently could quickly make the sidewalk impassable.

PRUNING AN OPEN SHRUB

A number of attractive shrubs provide vivid color in the fall in the Southwest. For early autumn color, plant chamisa with purple aster. The combination of purple and yellow is one of the more exciting combinations I have seen anywhere. Gambel's and Schumard oak will provide some of the type of color common back east, although they are smaller than the eastern oaks.

Golden current, threeleaf sumac, and littleleaf sumac are three of the brightest. Woodbine, or Virginia creeper, will add color to the landscape if given space to climb. Be sure to include some evergreens in the landscape to provide background and contrast to the other colors. In addition to the traditional conifers, some native broadleaf evergreens such as cliffrose, creosote bush, and fernbush can provide an easy-care screen from passing traffic and background for other shrubs on a large lot.

Several shrubs do well in hot, dry conditions. Yuccas and agaves can tolerate such conditions. Members of the *Artemisia* genus can generally tolerate heat and need little water. Most are evergreen, although they are gray-green or blue-green. Cliffrose is another possibility for those conditions. It has dark green leaves and will grow to be a rugged-looking six-foot shrub, although it does grow slowly.

Junipers are among the most common evergreen shrubs. Most junipers can tolerate hot, dry conditions. When selecting junipers consider their mature size. Many common junipers like pfitzers, Hollywood junipers, and others grow to extremely large plants over several years. Junipers come in hundreds of varieties. The Andorra juniper, some of the Japanese junipers, and others are smaller and lower-growing than the older varieties.

Creeping mahonia or creeping barberry is a good low-growing shrub for shady areas where a barrier plant is needed. A native of the New Mexico mountains, it grows well in dry shade. It has stiff holly-like leaves and stays green all winter. It will not grow tall enough to interfere with people seeing oncoming traffic across a corner but will discourage people from walking across the area. A few strategically placed large rocks could complete the mountain look and further discourage pedestrian traffic. If there is sun at the edges of the area, try some of the new low-growing shrub roses where they will get five or more hours of sun per day. They also grow only one to two feet tall and are thorny enough to discourage foot traffic.

The Siberian pea shrub would be a good selection for a tall barrier hedge. It is a dense, somewhat thorny shrub that can grow fifteen to twenty feet tall. It can be sheared as a hedge or left unpruned. The leaves are pale green compound leaves, much like honey locust leaves. The bushes have yellow flowers in the spring and pea pod–like fruit that develops in late summer. Siberian pea shrub is a cold-hardy shrub that can be grown even at the highest altitudes in the Southwest. It does well in poor soils because it forms a relationship with soil bacteria that fix nitrogen. The bark on the twigs splits to create interesting patterns, and there are spines where the leaves join the twigs.

To make overgrown lilac shrubs look better in late summer, cut out enough of the outside growth for access to the inside, then remove all the dead wood. After the plants flower in the spring, cut out all the old, gnarled canes and all but eight or ten younger canes. Scratch a cup of 20-20-10 or similar fertilizer into the soil or mulch with aged manure. There will be fewer flowers next spring, but the following spring the lilac will come back stronger than ever.

Some lilacs take longer to start flowering after they are transplanted than others. Some individual plants may take years to flower. There are several ways to try to get a lilac to flower. Start by watering heavily in late summer when the flower buds are forming. Leave the water running slowly

Spring Flowering Shrubs

Forsythia
Flowering Quince
Flowering Almond
Bush cherries and plums
Barberry
Dogwoods
Most viburnums
Deutzia
Kerria
Beauty bush
Honeysuckle
Mock orange
Pomegranate
Rose acacia
New Mexico locust
Spirea

Summer Flowering Shrubs

Butterfly bush
Lilac
Crape myrtle
Caryopteris
Rose of Sharon
Hybiscus
Hydrangea
Privet
Shrub roses
Elderberries
Vitex
Weigela
Russian sage
Blue mist
Bird of Paradise
Pyracantha
Oleander

under the lilac for several hours so the water soaks into the soil quite deeply. If there are no flowers the next spring, thin out some of the branches at the base of the plant. The next year try root pruning. Dig a two-foot ditch around the plants, mix the soil with a generous amount of superphosphate (about eight ounces for every three feet of ditch), and return the soil to the ditch. With this drastic treatment the lilac generally reacts as though it is about to die and will produce some flowers in an attempt to preserve the species.

Crepe myrtle in colder areas of the Southwest is likely to freeze back when the winters are cold. Fortunately their flowers are borne on new wood so they will flower even if they freeze all the way back to the ground. The easiest thing to do is to accept a crepe myrtle shrub and enjoy the lovely flowers. To protect it and make it grow into a tree, plant it in a protected patio area or build a wire cage around it and fill the cage with leaves. The leaves will insulate the plant and keep it from freezing back.

All willows, pussy willow included, prefer plenty of moisture and soils with lower pH than many southwestern soils, although they are somewhat adaptable. They are susceptible to many insects and diseases. Pussy willows should be pruned only in late spring, although a few branches can be taken inside for forcing in midwinter. To force bouquets of flowering shrubs to bloom early indoors, cut branches of the tree or shrub after the buds have started to swell, bring them inside, and allow them to open. Some of the best flowering plants for forcing are forsythia, flowering quince, cherry, apple, peach, plum, including the ornamental varieties, and flowering almond. Some of the early flowering natives can also be forced. Check to see if their buds are swelling before bringing them inside. Later-flowering shrubs will not open inside because their flower buds are not fully developed yet. Do not try to force lilac or other late spring or early summer shrubs.

If a pussy willow shrub is large, healthy, and unpruned but still doesn't have fuzzy flowers it may be a female rather than a male plant. In the

Common Female and Juvenile Juniper Varieties
(plant these to avoid pollen problems)

Alpina

Ames

Arcadia

Blue acrea

Blue carpet

Blue Point

Blue vase Texas star

Buffalo

Canareti

Chinensis prostrata

Cologreen

Cupressifolia

Douglasii

Emerald sentinel

Emerson

Expansa

Fairview

Filicina

Glenmore

Green columnar

Grey owl

Hetzii (sometimes labeled Pfitzer, which is a male variety)

Horizontalis glauca

Horizontalis prostrata

Horizontalis variegata

Kaizuka

Keteleerii

Livingston

Maney

Marcella

Meyeri

Mint julep

Moffettii

Petraea

Planifolia

Robusta

Sargentii

Sea green

Skandia

Spartan

Spearmint

Table top

Tularosa

Virginiana pendula

Wilton carpet

Wiltonii

true pussy willow, only the males produce the soft, furry catkins we grow them for. Generally only male plants are sold. If flowers do not appear in the spring, cut the whole bush back to short stubs and let it grow new vigorous shoots. If those shoots do not produce flowers replace the shrub.

The oleander is a shrub that is hardy only down to about 10°F. It will freeze back or freeze out completely in most of the Southwest but will survive in the southern areas. In other areas, it can be grown as a large pot plant that is brought indoors in winter. Oleanders have attractive flowers in shades of pink, red, and white. All parts of the plant are poisonous if consumed. Even the smoke from burning branches is toxic, and people have died after eating hot dogs roasted on oleander branches.

Boxwood is a fine-textured broadleaf evergreen that is often used in formal gardens and sheared to topiary shapes. Among the several varieties of boxwood, only two are likely to be available in nurseries and only one, the littleleaf boxwood, is likely to survive in most of the Southwest. It grows to a height of three to four feet and spreads three to four feet. The common boxwood, which grows to a height of fifteen to twenty feet, may also be available. Both boxwoods will do better in partial shade and require cool, moist soil. A heavy organic mulch is almost essential for a healthy boxwood in hot dry areas. Boxwoods do not do well in areas that have extremes of summer heat or winter cold. The common boxwood is more sensitive to these extremes than littleleaf boxwood. Even the littleleaf boxwood will not do well if it gets strong afternoon sun or reflection off rocks or light-colored soils. In cold winters the leaves of the littleleaf boxwood will turn yellow-brown rather than staying true green. Over time boxwoods will decline under the conditions of climate and soil we have here and will need to be replaced.

VINES

In a space less than three feet wide, a vine growing on a wall or trellis can provide shade or a barrier. Some vigorous vines to consider are passion vine, Virginia creeper, and silver lace vine. If a barrier plant with thorns is desired, hardy climbing roses will effectively cover a wall. Passion vine, silver lace vine, and climbing roses will need some support to begin growing up the wall. Passion vine and silver lace vine have tendrils that will cling to the support; the roses will have to be tied to the support. Virginia creeper can cling to the wall without any support structure.

Virginia creeper and passion vine are the most vigorous growers. They spread by underground suckers, and if growing conditions are right they may come up several feet from where they are planted. This will be less of a problem if they are confined by a wall and a sidewalk, but both passion vine and Virginia Creeper can cross under sidewalks and come up on the other side if there is water or more fertile soil there.

Getting rid of established vines like English ivy or Virginia creeper is quite difficult. Pull them up and chop out roots whenever they come up. Prevent development of full-grown leaves, and the plants will eventually be starved out. A safe chemical to use is glyphosate. The brand names are Roundup or Kleenup. Carefully apply the chemical to the leaves of the vine each time they appear. To apply it, put on a pair of rubber gloves, carefully moisten a sponge with the herbicide, and brush herbicide on the leaves. Do not get it on any other plants. It will kill anything that is green. Killing out the vine completely will take some time. Glyphosate is inactivated when it contacts the soil, so it will not contaminate water or soil.

CHAPTER 6

Fruit

GENERAL

Proper planning can increase the chances of successfully producing fruit
in the fickle southwestern climate. An orchard will do best on a gentle,
north-facing slope where the trees will flower later and the blossoms are
less likely to freeze. On a south- or west-facing slope, the sun will warm
the plants sooner and they will flower earlier, increasing the chance of
freeze damage. Cold air collects at the base of slopes, making late freezes
a problem, and the trees can be damaged by wind at the top of hills or
mountains.

Other things to consider for the placement of the orchard are the depth
of the soil, ease of watering, and ability to get equipment in to a large
orchard. The soil must be at least two, preferably three, feet deep. This
is sometimes a problem on slopes; to get sufficient soil depth, your orchard
may need to be on a flat area. Orchards on slopes are generally watered
with drip irrigation systems, which is more expensive than flood systems
but uses considerably less water. Mowers and other equipment are needed
in large home orchards, so access roads should be provided.

An excellent fruit crop in most of the Southwest is the exception rather
than the rule. More often than not the weather gets warm early, so buds
on the fruit trees start to break early; then it gets cold again and freezes
all those early buds. Some fruit production may occur in those years in

protected areas or in areas where the early warming did not occur (see climate zone map, p. 169).

If fruit does set on the trees, it can drop off for a number of reasons. Tiny, undeveloped fruit will drop because it did not get pollinated. Fruit trees that have set more fruit than the tree can support to maturity also have what is called a "June drop," which may or may not come in June. This is a natural thinning of a heavy crop of fruit so the tree can produce enough sugar to mature the remaining fruit. This is a beneficial process that produces larger and sweeter fruit. On peach and apple trees, the fruit may need to be further thinned after the natural fruit drop to get extra large, extra sweet fruit.

Leave about one peach or apple for every six to eight inches of stem, one apricot for every four to five inches of stem. The number of fruit a tree can support is determined by the number of leaves. For example, thirty-five leaves are needed to produce one peach. Spacing the fruit along the stem is easier than counting leaves.

Fruit trees take specialized pruning, although the first step of the process is the same as for any woody plant—remove dead or dying wood. A young fruit tree can be trained in several ways. Apples, pears, and cherries generally grow with a straight central trunk, or leader. These trees can be trained to have whorls of side or scaffold branches spaced evenly around the trunk with about six to ten inches vertically between the branches. The first whorl should be two to three feet off the ground. The next whorl should be three feet above that and the third, three feet above the second. Once a tree gets more than ten to twelve feet tall it is difficult to deal with in the home orchard, so it should be pruned to a modified central leader system. The central leader is cut off just above a more or less horizontal branch about six feet above the ground. This is the most common system in the Southwest for pears, cherries, and many apples. An open center system can be used for trees that have a natural vase-shaped form. To create an open center, the leader is cut off after five or six nicely spaced branches have formed three to four feet off the ground. Ideally the remaining scaffold branches form an angle of forty-five degrees or more from the trunk. Once the basic shape is formed, young fruit trees should be pruned as little as possible but should be shaped to maintain even growth on all sides and kept somewhat open to encourage the development of fruiting wood.

When the tree starts producing fruit, water sprouts and suckers should be cut out in the summer. Cracked, broken, or diseased branches should be removed whenever they appear. Other pruning should be done in late winter. If two branches are rubbing against each other or if two scaffold branches are crowding each other, remove one. Generally the lower one should be removed, but if the lower one is the healthier or more productive branch, leave it. Sunlight must get to all the leaves for the tree to be productive, so if the branching is too dense, thin the lateral branches to open the tree up. Branches that are too tall or too long can also be cut back.

Apples and pears bear fruit on spurs or on old wood, so be careful not to remove the spurs when pruning. Cherries produce fruit on spurs or one- to two-year-old wood. Apricots, plums, and their hybrids produce fruit on spurs and new wood, and peaches and nectarines produce fruit on new wood. When cutting back branches of apricots, plums, and peaches do not prune off all the flower buds.

Spring is sometimes upon us before we manage to get our trees pruned. If the trees were thoroughly pruned in previous years, it will do no harm to let them go unpruned one year. If the trees are severely overgrown or need shaping, they can still be pruned even in midspring. If the trees are pruned after they start flowering, some of those flowers, along with a large amount of leaf area, will be pruned off. The leaves produce the energy for the development of the fruit. The actual energy balance depends on a number of factors including water, soil fertility, and how much fruit was produced the previous summer. If the tree doesn't have enough energy to ripen the fruit that is left after pruning, it will send up water sprouts, or suckers, which are fast-growing sprouts with large leaves on them. Cut these sprouts off in late summer after the fruit is ripe.

The most serious danger to young fruit trees in the Southwest is the weather. Sudden temperature drops in the fall, warming, then freezing again in the spring, or extreme summer heat can damage fruit trees. Proper irrigation and fertilization can increase a fruit tree's chances of surviving the extremes of life in the Southwest. Once the buds begin to swell, the root zone of fruit trees should be kept slightly damp. Water deeply enough to moisten the top thirty inches of the soil. To determine the depth, irrigate the trees for half an hour, then dig a small hole to determine how deeply the soil is moist. Use that depth to determine the time needed for the water to penetrate thirty inches. For example, if the water penetrated ten inches in half an hour, water for one and a half hours to get the water to penetrate thirty inches. If it penetrated only three inches, water five hours to moisten the top thirty inches. The frequency of watering depends on the texture of the soil. On clay soils, once a month may be sufficient except in the hottest weather; sandy soils will need water more frequently. On all soils, water more frequently in extremely hot weather. Reduce the frequency of watering gradually, starting in August, to encourage the plants to become dormant early. This will help them resist early freezes. Water the trees about once a month in winter to keep them from drying out completely.

Fruit tree blossoms can withstand temperatures down to about 30°F for brief periods of time without any damage. If the temperatures are predicted to go lower than that, begin spraying the tree with water as the temperature falls below freezing. As the water freezes, heat is released into the branch. This will save the fruit down to about 27°F. Keep spraying until the temperatures again rise above freezing or all the effort will have been wasted. If the temperature falls below 27°F for a few hours, the fruit will freeze even with the water treatment.

One way to slightly delay the opening of the blossoms is to sprinkle the trees during the warmest part of the day on the warmest days of late winter. This keeps the plant cooler because of the water evaporation, thus delaying the opening of the buds slightly. This slight delay may be enough to avoid some of the later freezes.

Some fruits are more susceptible to freeze than others. Peaches, for example will freeze at higher temperatures than apples. The earliest flowering trees, like apricot, are most likely to freeze.

Within two weeks after flowering, the fruit should be developing. Look at the base of places where the petals fell off. If there is small fruit there, take a few of them and split them with a thumbnail or knife. Look for dark bands inside the fruit. If there is small fruit and it does not have dark bands inside it the fruit has set.

Fertilizer should be applied only in the spring and early summer. Apply about one pound of fertilizer for every inch in diameter of the trunk. Divide the total amount of fertilizer into three parts, and apply one part when the trees have just broken dormancy, one part in late May, and the last part in late June. Do not apply any nitrogen fertilizer after the first of July. Excess nitrogen, like excess water, can delay dormancy of trees. If a tree is not fully dormant when the temperatures first get really cold, it is much more likely to be injured by the cold.

Rodents can seriously damage the bark of young fruit trees. If the damage is aboveground the rodents are most likely rabbits, whereas belowground teeth marks were probably made by mice. Both can be reduced or prevented by placing a barrier around the tree. Remove all the grass and weeds next to the tree to eliminate nesting and hiding places for rodents, then wrap the trunk with fine mesh hardware cloth or plastic tree guards. Be sure to use solid tree guards. Some tree guards have holes in them and the mice climb in and make their nests right next to the food supply. The barrier should reach at least eighteen inches above the ground to prevent rabbit damage and two inches below the ground to prevent mouse damage.

APPLES

Many varieties of apples are available to home gardeners. Some good disease-resistant varieties include Freedom, Jonafree, Nova Easygrow, Priscilla, Redfree, and Spartan. Apples require a certain number of hours at temperatures below 45°F to produce fruit. In the low desert areas of the region, low-chill apples can be used for a more consistent crop. Low-chill apples for the warmest part of the region include Anna, Beverly Hills, Granny Smith, and Winter Banana. This is not an exhaustive list of apple varieties that can be grown in the Southwest. Apple varieties available at nurseries or in catalogs are generally those that grow well under a variety of conditions. Don't be afraid to try older varieties from local sources; they may do well under the specific conditions of your area.

The most common problem apples have is worms that are the larvae of codling moth. The codling moth overwinters in sheltered places on or near the apple tree. Many of them overwinter in loose bark on the tree, but if there is debris under the tree, a significant number will overwinter there. Clean up all fallen apples and leaves under the tree and destroy them. When pruning, remove the branches and twigs from the orchard or yard. Also clean up the area around cherry, pear, apricot, peach, plum, or nut trees. Codling moths prefer apples but can also be found on other fruit trees. Spray with dormant oil in early spring when night temperatures are expected to stay above freezing and day temperatures are not expected to exceed 80°F.

If no control measures are taken, as much as 95 percent of the crop is likely to be wormy. Moths can be trapped as described below, or you can begin spraying as soon as the petals fall from the blossoms and continue spraying every week to ten days. Use either a manufactured pesticide that is labeled for controlling codling moth on apples or the plant-derived pesticide Ryania. Ryania is one of the more toxic organic pesticides, although it is not toxic to humans or other warm-blooded animals.

Codling moths are quite difficult to control without using chemicals.

Irradiated male moths have been released in large orcharding areas. These moths mate with females and no offspring are produced. This method is quite effective in major fruit producing areas but not useful to the backyard gardener.

A knowledge of the life cycle of the coddling moth will help in choosing control methods. The larvae pupate in the spring and emerge in two to three weeks. The moths then mate and lay eggs on leaves, twigs, and fruit spurs. Six to twenty days after the eggs are laid the worms hatch out and crawl along the twigs to burrow into the apples. *Bacillus thuringiensis* (BT), the bacteria that is effective against most moth larvae, does not work well on coddling moth larvae unless it is applied after the larvae have hatched and before they enter the apple, a very brief period of time. Pheromone, or sex attractant, traps are used to determine when the moths are flying and therefore when chemical or organic sprays would be most effective. Pheromone traps are used by some organic orchardists as a control measure. Because they trap only a small portion of the male moths, they are not particularly effective when used on a small scale. Although cleaning up under the tree, dormant oil, pheromone traps, and BT will reduce the population, they will not eliminate codling moths.

Delicious apples grown in the Southwest don't always look like Delicious apples. In most areas of the Northwest and Midwest, Delicious apples naturally produce pronounced protuberances, or bumps, on the calyx end.

Apple Varieties for the Southwest

Freedom
Jonafree
Nova Easygrow
Priscilla
Redfree
Spartan

Low chill apples for warmer areas

Anna
Beverly Hills
Granny Smith
Winter Banana

This is not an exhaustive list of apple varieties that can be grown in the southwest.

In other areas, the apples are sprayed with a substance called Promalin to cause them to have the characteristic shape that people identify with Delicious apples. Without this chemical spray, the apples are less cone shaped and more rounded on the end. It does not affect the quality or taste of the apple and is done only because people generally identify apples by shape and color.

BLUEBERRIES

Blueberries require a soil with a pH of about 4.5. Since most soil in the Southwest has a pH above 7.0 growing blueberries here is difficult, but outlet stores continue to sell them. Most people don't consider it worth the trouble, but it is possible to create a blueberry bed. First, remove all the soil from the selected planting area to a depth of eighteen inches. Replace the soil with a mix of equal parts sand, peat moss, and compost. Add about half a pound of wettable sulfur per forty square feet of bed and mix it in well. Then plant the blueberries, give them plenty of water, and mulch the soil well. Blueberry roots are shallow so do not cultivate around the plants.

About a month after planting, have the soil tested. If the pH is above 5.0, sprinkle more sulfur on top of the soil. Blueberries need an annual application of nitrogen. Probably the best source is ammonium sulfate since it helps acidify the soil. Test the pH of the soil each spring and add additional sulfur if it is above 5.0. Our slightly alkaline water may raise the pH in the bed. Do not use nitrates on blueberries as they are toxic to the plants. Don't add phosphorous or potassium unless the soil has very low levels.

Blueberries use lots of water. It is best to create a sunken bed at least two inches deep, then fill that with water once a week. Placing the beds in an area where they will receive afternoon shade will help the blueberries survive our hot dry weather. A light pruning in early spring will keep the plants in shape.

Highbush or rabbiteye blueberries are the best choices for this area.

Highbush can survive colder temperatures than rabbiteye. A rabbiteye variety should be planted in a sheltered place. Remove some of the flower buds from a highbush variety each year to get a crop of flavorful, large berries. The flower buds are larger and rounder than leaf buds. Either strip them off or remove some of the twigs with a large number of flower buds.

BRAMBLES

Blackberries and raspberries are understory plants in wooded areas and therefore are not well adapted to much of the Southwest, but they can be grown here with proper care. They do quite well in the mountains. In other areas they should be planted where they are shaded part of the day and the soil remains cool. Mulching the soil will help them become established.

Raspberries and blackberries send up offshoots or little plants next to the main plant. Look under each of the plants to see if there are any offshoots. These can be dug up and moved to new locations. First use the shovel to cut the root the new plant sprouted from, then dig up the plant with as many of its own roots as you can. Plant it in a new location and water it well.

The plants can also be layered to start more new plants. Take a cane (branch) of the raspberry plant and bend it over. Scratch or cut the bottom of the cane where it touches the ground. A rooting hormone applied to the spot where the cane was scratched is useful but not required. Cover the cane with two or three inches of soil. Keep the soil moist during the summer. Roots will grow from the cane. In the spring dig up the cane and transplant it.

CHERRIES

New sweet cherry varieties are not developed as rapidly as new varieties of some other fruits. Good light-colored varieties include Emperor Francis, Gold, Napoleon (Queen Anne), and Rainier. Dark-colored choices include Bing, Cavalier, Hedelfingen, Sam, Schmidt, Stella, Van, Vega, Vista, and Windsor. Sweet cherries need a pollinator, so make sure another sweet cherry variety is planted nearby.

Often sweet cherries will have little maggots in them. The maggots are the larvae of the cherry fruit fly. The insects overwinter in the soil in small, hard brown cases called puparia. The flies emerge from the ground during June or July and fly about in the sun for a few days, feeding on moisture or honeydew on the trees. The females lay eggs in the cherries, piercing the fruit with their ovipositors and depositing the eggs in the flesh. The very small, white maggots hatch in a week or less and immediately begin to feed close to the pit. They can feed for as much as two weeks before there is any outward sign that the cherries are infested. The maggots are so small at the early stages they are not easily seen. When they are fully grown, the maggots exit from the cherries. The fruit may be shriveled on one side and small holes may appear. The maggots drop to the ground and form their puparia a few inches beneath the surface. They remain there until the following spring.

Chemically controlling cherry fruit flies requires several regularly scheduled sprays of Diazinon. Since the flies all emerge during a relatively short period of time, a trapping program can determine when they are emerging; insecticides can be used only when the flies are present, rather than continuously spraying in the hope of killing some flies. Using several traps in one tree to catch the flies before they lay eggs in the fruit is a biological control method. Picking up all fruit that drops and cultivating the top few inches of soil under the trees in the fall will also help control the insects. Cherry fruit fly traps are available at local nurseries and through organic pest control catalogs.

FIGS

Some figs are more tender than others. Celeste (or Celestial), Brown Turkey, or Texas Everbearing varieties should survive winters in the southern and central parts of the region nicely with protection. Kadota is the most commonly sold fig variety in the area, but it actually bears best in the hot central valleys of California. It is raised commercially for canning, so the fruit color and texture is closer to what many people think a fig should be. It can overwinter if well protected. Other varieties are extremely cold sensitive and take long periods of heat to produce fruit.

To protect a young tree in an exposed area, mound some soil around the base as around a tender rose, then build a wire cage around the entire tree and fill it with leaves, straw, or wadded up newspaper. This will insulate the tree from the worst of the winter cold and winds.

When the tree gets too large for this treatment, mound and cage the base and wrap the upper branches in insulating blankets or many layers of newspaper. Or leave the upper portion of the tree unprotected and let it freeze back. The fig will be a large shrub rather than a tree, but it will produce one crop of fruit each year at the end of the summer and will require less work than trying to protect a full-size fig tree from the cold.

GRAPES

Grapevines bear leaves and fruit on slender, woody canes that grow from brown fuzzy buds each year. The base of each leaf has a bud. Left unpruned, grapevines soon extend to enormous lengths with a tangle of leaves and vines at the edge and a core of unproductive wood. Containing grapevines to an arbor is a challenge. The cane pruning, or head trained, method will provide shade as well as grapes. Start by selecting seven to ten smooth young canes that come from the woody part of the grapevine close to the top of the arbor. Tie ribbons or markers around those canes so they are not lost during the pruning process. Next, cut everything else off. Start by cutting the woody trunk just above the last of the selected canes. Remove and discard that wood. Cut off any side branches below the selected canes, then remove the remaining new canes. If any of the original selected canes were broken in the pruning process, cut them back to two buds. This should leave seven to nine healthy canes starting from approximately the same location. Select four of these canes to be the producing canes for the next season. Leave ten buds on each of those four canes, cutting off and discarding the portion of the cane beyond those ten buds. The other canes should be cut back to two buds to act as renewal spurs the following year.

The next year the form of the vine will already be established, and it will be easier to prune the vines in this manner. Each spring, prune to four canes with ten buds and three to five renewal spurs. Grapes grown solely for production should be pruned differently. Contact your county agent for more advice.

Fruit may fail to develop for a number of reasons. Cold temperatures just as the flowers were opening or the fruit was beginning to develop is one cause. Another cause is lack of pollination. Grapes are pollinated by wind and by insects. However grape pollen is extremely light and fluffy. Extremely high winds can blow away the pollen before it has a chance to pollinate the fruit. Insects cannot fly in extremely high winds either. Other causes could be temperatures over one hundred degrees for a prolonged period of time or poor production of pollen because the soil was too dry in early spring. A few varieties of grapes need a pollinator, although most varieties are self-fruitful. A pollinator is another variety of grape that flowers at about the same time. It should be placed within several hundred feet of the variety needing the pollinator.

PEACHES AND NECTARINES

Peaches, one of the oldest known cultivated fruits, come in many varieties. Nectarines were developed from a branch of a peach tree that produced "fuzzless peaches." The only difference between a nectarine and a peach is the fuzz on the skin. Most peaches and nectarines have yellow flesh but a few have white flesh. The white-fleshed varieties are more strongly flavored and are best for eating straight from the tree. They also tend to have hardier buds and may survive winter freezes better than yellow-fleshed peaches in the northern part of the region. Some white-fleshed varieties include Babcock, Belle of Georgia, Champion, Gold Mine (nectarine), Melba, Oldmixon Free, Raritan Rose, and Red Chief (nectarine). Red Haven, Redskin, and all varieties derived from the Elberta peach are the most popular yellow-skinned varieties.

Be prepared to prop up the branches with boards or forked branches if they seem to be too heavily loaded with peaches. Even if the fruit crop is thinned, developing peaches could become so heavy they break the branches of the peach tree.

Peaches will drip a sticky resin any time their surface is injured. This can be caused by hail, birds, or insects. Codling moths attack peaches as well as apples. They lay their eggs just below the surface of the peach. When the eggs hatch, the larvae feed on the inside of the peach. Once the worms are in the peaches there is no way to kill them and still have an edible peach. If wormy peaches have been a problem in previous years start a preventative spray program just after the blossoms fall. Use traps to determine when moths are present, then spray with one of the pesticides recommended for codling moth on fruit.

Borers are the most common insect pest for peach trees. Immediately after planting peach trees, dig a shallow trench all the way around the trunk about four inches away. Pour mothballs or borer crystals made of paradichlorobenzene into the trench, then cover them with soil. This will fumigate the soil and keep the borers out. The procedure should be repeated every year to keep the tree free from borers.

The same treatment can also be used on mature peach, plum, cherry, and apricot trees that have not already been girdled by borers. Examine the bark just below the soil line. If borers have not damaged more than half the trunk, surround it with moth crystals. Cover the crystals with about two inches of soil.

NUTS

Black walnuts, Carpathian walnuts, and pecans are the most common nuts grown in the Southwest. Black walnuts and Carpathian walnuts, which are like English walnuts, produce their heaviest crop in the central part of New Mexico. Black walnuts will fall off the tree over a long period of time during late fall and early winter. Pick them up as they fall, remove the husks, then let them dry for two to three weeks before storing them in a cool, dry place. After all the leaves fall, some walnuts may remain on the tree. These can be shaken or knocked down with a pole. To remove the husks from black walnuts, place the nuts on a driveway and drive a car over them. The broken husks can then be pulled off and the nuts spread on a flat surface to dry. (The shells of Carpathian walnuts are too thin for this procedure.) Be sure to wear gloves while removing the husks to avoid staining your hands. To store the dried nuts, put them in a bag, basket, or other container and store them in a closet or garage, away from leaks or other possible sources of moisture. They can also be cracked and stored in plastic bags in the freezer, which is more convenient.

Several pests have the potential to damage the pecan industry, so the New Mexico Department of Agriculture has put a quarantine on nut trees. Pecans and other nut trees must be fumigated before being shipped into New Mexico to prevent insects from being imported into the state. One of these pests, the pecan nut casebearer, is very damaging to pecans. The moths produce two generations per year, and each larva of the second generation can eat three to four immature pecans. Fortunately, we do not have pecan nut casebearers in New Mexico. Other insects, such as the pecan weevil and hickory shuckworm, can also be imported on pecans.

CHAPTER 7

Flowers

PLANNING AND PREPARING THE FLOWER BED

The first step in planning a flower bed is to determine the points from which the bed will be viewed. Will the bed be visible through a window from inside the house, or will it be viewed strictly from outside? Will it be viewed from a patio or frequently used lawn area or from the street? Locate the bed in an area of high visibility. At the same time, keep in mind such factors as soil type and drainage. Plan the bed so it will be attractive from all the major viewing points throughout the season.

Make a drawing of the area where the bed will be planted, putting in trees, the house, and other permanent features. Then sketch in the space you will be using for the bed. Will it be a formal rectangular or circular design or an informal curved bed? Be sure to leave at least eighteen inches between the house and the bed. This will serve as a walkway from which the flowers can be tended in the back of a wide bed and will also protect the walls and foundation. Indicate any high or low spots on the drawing.

Next, determine the soil type or types. Is it clay or sand, or both clay and sand? In many areas of the Southwest, sand gives way to clay rather abruptly, or layers of sand are found on top of layers of clay. Dig a hole at least two feet deep to determine if the soil is uniform to that depth or if different soil types are layered. If the soil is layered close to the surface, either mix the layers, if possible, with a rototiller or by digging, or dig a few holes through a hard lower layer to improve drainage. At the same time mix some organic matter into the soil. If the soil is uniform, till organic matter into the first six to eight inches.

Intensive gardening makes more sense in the Southwest than almost anywhere else. An intensive garden bed is one in which the entire sur-face of the soil is covered with plants when they reach mature size. Unlike in many other places, intensive beds in the Southwest should be sunken rather than raised.

To prepare an intensive bed, first remove sod and weeds from a space narrow enough that you can reach across it and long enough to provide the garden space required. If the weeds don't have a lot of seeds on them, put them in the compost pile. Remove the topsoil if it has better color or texture than the lower soil and save it for use later. Next, dig out about eight inches of soil and use it to make a dike around the bed. If the bed is next to the house, leave a path at least a foot wide between the house and the bed and build up that side a little more than the other sides.

To condition the soil, add about six inches of compost or manure on top of the bed, then put the saved topsoil back in. Now the work really begins. Dig an eighteen-inch trench along one side of the bed. Put this soil in a cart or wheelbarrow and take it to the other end of the bed. Then dig out the next shovel width to a depth of eighteen inches and put that in the original trench. Thoroughly mix compost or manure as the soil is moved. Fill that trench with the soil next to it, and so on, to reach the other end of the bed, where the trench should be filled with the soil in the wheelbarrow. This process cannot be done as effectively with a rototiller because the rototiller does not mix the material in to a depth of eighteen inches. Once a bed is prepared in this way, however, it can be kept in good condition for three to five years by tilling in a three-inch layer of compost each fall.

Don't put any mulch on the annual beds in the fall. If they are left bare, they will warm up earlier in the spring. In the spring get the soil tested and add any fertilizers you might need, then begin planting. As

SUNKEN BED   RAISED BED

soon as weeds start to sprout, put a heavy mulch on the bed, but don't let it touch any of the plants until they are big and tough enough to resist the sow bugs and fungi that might be lurking in the mulch. A three- to six-inch layer of mulch will effectively discourage almost all weeds.

If the soil freezes solid, put a heavy layer of mulch on all the hardy perennials. This acts as insulation to keep the soil frozen. Unmulched soil is likely to freeze and thaw, at least at the surface, several times during the winter. Each time the soil freezes and thaws, it moves a little, which can damage the roots of perennials and sometimes even heave the crowns of the plants right out of the soil, leaving the roots behind. If the soil stays frozen, the plants will be healthier and stronger in the spring.

When creating a flower bed, choose from three classes of bedding plants: annuals, perennials, and drought-tolerant plants. The drought-tolerant plants can be either annuals or perennials but are listed as a separate class because they should not be mixed with plants needing more water. The most common annual bedding plants include marigolds, petunias, geraniums, begonias, impatiens, salvia, vinca, and zinnias. Begonias and impatiens prefer shade, whereas the others should be grown in full sun. Easy-care perennials include dianthus, snapdragons, delphinium, poppies, baby's breath, hollyhock, and a variety of bulbs. Perennials do not have to be replanted each year, but they generally have a shorter flowering season so more planning is required to have a full summer of flowers. Some of the easiest-care bedding plants, especially if the bed is on the south or west side of the house, are the drought-tolerant ones. These include verbena, purple aster, butterfly weed, chocolate flower, purple coneflower, snow-in-summer, gayfeather, blue flax, California poppy, and some penstemons.

When selecting bedding plants, choose colors that go well with each other and with the color of your house. They should not disappear against the wall, as white flowers in front of white walls do, but the colors should not clash either. Don't choose tall plants like delphinium or hollyhock if they are to be planted in front of a window, and plan the heights of the plants so each plant will be visible when it flowers. Look up the mature height, spread, and appearance of the plants in a catalog or garden book. Place taller plants in the back of the bed and shorter plants in front. Use a variety of forms and textures to create a pleasing effect. Delphiniums are tall plants with columnar forms that might be effective in the back of a border, for example, while dianthus has a low, mounding form that is attractive in front.

Select a color scheme. A bed could be all one color, have two or three complementary colors, or be multicolored. Another option is to have a bed that changes color through the season. One possibility is to start with red flowers in early spring, followed by pink and blue, then red and orange summer flowers and white or purple flowers in the fall.

Determine the bloom time of all the flowers so you have blooms from early spring through fall. In a small bed, choose plants that are attractive over a long period of time, such as yarrow, dianthus, daylily, gaillardia, English lavender, chrysanthemum, and coneflower. In a larger bed, include a larger variety of flowers, some of which may have shorter bloom periods.

When the plan is complete, with height, spread, color, and texture of the plants all in balance, it is time to buy and plant the flowers. Some catalogs sell preplanned flower beds with all the plants needed to complete the theme. Be sure to purchase strong, healthy nursery stock and plant it properly. Check the catalog or consult with nursery staff for planting instructions. After the plants are established, place a heavy layer of organic mulch around them. Mulch will reduce the amount of water required in summer and protect the plants from the effects of freezing and thawing in the winter. Apply a new layer of mulch each spring as soon as the weather really warms up and in early winter as soon as it gets really cold.

Take care of the flower bed in the fall to produce a successful garden the next year. Remove all the plant material from the perennial bed as soon as it has died or frozen. Put any plants that are not diseased in the compost pile. Burn or discard diseased material. Dig the roots or bulbs of any tender perennials and store them in a cool, dry place, packing them in sand or sawdust to keep them from getting dehydrated before spring. Be careful when top growth is removed from the perennials. In some cases, the old growth remains firmly attached to the roots even though it has died; in other cases, next year's tender new growth is already close to the surface. Gently rake the bed with a leaf rake, then cut any growth that is left rather than pulling it out.

Most well-established perennials or bulbs can survive short periods of subfreezing weather quite easily after they have come up. A few more tender perennials may be damaged by freezing weather. Extremely cold weather in late spring can damage plants. Protect actively growing plants by piling snow on top of them. If snow is not available, a heavy covering of organic mulch applied before the weather turns really cold will serve the same purpose. Remove it carefully as the weather begins to get warmer.

ANNUALS

The average frost-free date in Albuquerque is April 20. In most valley locations, such as Corrales, the average last-frost date is later. The average last-frost date in the northeast heights is earlier. According to weather data over the past forty years, the earliest planting dates in the city are usually found in the area between Wyoming and Juan Tabo and between Lomas and Montgomery, except for a few protected microclimates in the older parts of the heights.

The last-frost date is considerably more difficult to predict in the Southwest than it is in places with more stable climates. Our growing season varies from one year to the next. The last frost may be in late March, April, or May. To be on the safe side, plan to set out tender plants about two weeks after the date shown on the map on page 162. Some can be set out a few weeks earlier, but keep others in reserve to plant when all danger of frost has passed.

Annual flowers can easily be started from seed, even seed saved from the previous year. Simply remove the heads of the flowers after they have gone to seed and are thoroughly dry. Examine the seeds and discard any that are moldy or infested with insects. Place the good seeds in a covered container to protect them from mice and insects. If the flowers are hybrids, do not save the seed. Some hybrids are sterile. They may produce seed but the seed will not grow. Other hybrids will set viable seeds, but the flowers growing from those seeds will not be the same as the hybrid from which they were collected.

Store seeds in a cool, dark, dry place. Temperatures just above freezing are best, although seeds are not injured by freezing temperatures. A garage or storage shed is a good place for storing the seeds over the winter. The refrigerator is the correct temperature, but it is too moist for long-term seed storage. Many seeds remain viable for long periods of time even under less than ideal conditions.

Marigolds and several other annual flowers reseed themselves readily in the garden. They are easy to control by removing all the flowers heads before they go to seed. If those flowers are desired in a section of the garden again, allow them to go to seed, then thin the reseeded plants so they are spaced at least six to eight inches apart. The extra seedlings can be discarded or transplanted to some other part of the yard.

Plants have developed several mechanisms to prevent their seeds from germinating at the wrong times in their natural environments. Some plants, like delphinium, require a cold period before they will germinate. Put the seeds in the refrigerator for about three weeks before planting them, and they should germinate readily. This process is called stratification. It prevents seeds from germinating in the fall in areas where the tender plants could freeze in the winter.

Some seeds require light to germinate. Oriental poppies are among this group. Lettuce, too, requires light for germination. The seeds that require light are frequently small and do not have enough stored food to support the tiny plant as it works its way up through a thick layer of soil. As a general rule, plant seed about twice as deep as the size of the seed. For light-loving varieties just sprinkle them on top of the soil, then be sure the soil surface does not dry out until the seeds have germinated. Other plants, onions for instance, need darkness for germination. These seeds should be planted slightly deeper to insure good germination.

Some seeds may need scarification before they germinate. Nick the seed coat with a file, nail clippers, or acid. The natural process of germination of these seeds starts when they are eaten by animals then dropped on the soil prepackaged with fertilizer for their early growth. They generally have very hard seed coats. Morning glory seeds will germinate more readily with scarification, although some people think they germinate too readily even without it.

Many plants from arid areas produce seeds with germination inhibitors in their seed coats; these inhibitors must be washed away before the seed will germinate. This prevents germination unless there is enough rainfall to ensure that the plants can survive. Many native plants will benefit from an overnight soaking in water before planting.

Seed packets should give any special instructions required for the germination of that type of seed. If the seeds have been saved or collected, check catalogs, library references, or the backs of seed packets in stores to see if the plant has any special needs.

When buying bedding plants, get small plants that do not have masses of roots coming out the bottom of the pot or cell pack. When planting them, be sure the planting hole is large enough to accommodate the existing root system. Remove the plant from the container, use your fingers or a light washing with the hose to loosen the roots, then plant them immediately. After planting, remove all the flowers from the plants so the roots can establish themselves. The plants will produce more flowers later and will be stronger and healthier if they are able to put all their energy into root development. The exception to this rule is flowers like celosia, or cockscomb, which produce only one flower head in their lifetime. If that flower head is removed the plant will not produce a new one. Buy those plants without any flowers on them so they have time to grow and develop strong stems and many leaves before they flower.

If cutworms are a problem, put little paper collars around the stems of plants as they are planted. The collar should extend from just below to just above ground level. Cutworms need to get their bodies around the stem to cut it off and the paper collars prevent this. Paper collars do not protect against white grubs. White grubs eat the roots of plants. If they were effectively controlled in the previous year, they may not be much of a problem on flowers, although it is a good idea to watch carefully for June beetles. White grubs are a serious problem on lawns. See chapter 4 for life cycle and control information.

Several annuals withstand heat well and can be used as transition plants between a lawn and Xeriscaped area. Some that might be useful are cockscomb, dusty miller, globe amaranth, marigold, petunia, portulaca, salvia, verbena, and zinnia. All these would need more water than many native plants but less than the lawn.

Verbena is the name of a family of plants that contains about three thousand species and a genus of plants that contains about two hundred species. Some verbenas are hybridized, or improved, plants. These are available through seed stores, nurseries, and catalogs. They are generally rather drought-tolerant but need to be watered regularly throughout the summer to grow and flower. Most verbena are annuals that may come back after mild winters. They come in a variety of bright and pastel colors ranging from deep blue and purple through violet and pink to white.

Native varieties of verbena that are used as cultivated plants need less water than the improved varieties but may still need to be irrigated, depending on their place of origin and where they are being grown. If they were collected locally, count on their being able to survive on local rainfall, but water them to encourage more prolific flowering. One plant in this category, called sand verbena, is really not a verbena at all. It is related to four-o-clocks.

The verbena family also includes some weeds. One definition of a weed is "a plant growing where you don't want it," so any verbena could be a weed. But the flowers of some verbenas are not attractive enough for anyone to want them in the garden. These verbenas are generally low-growing, square-stemmed plants with small purple flowers. They are easily removed by pulling or hoeing.

Sweet peas are a beautiful flower but sometimes difficult to grow in the Southwest. Success with sweet peas will depend on the spring weather, which is anything but predictable in the Southwest. You can do some things to make success more likely. First, select a location where the plants will get morning but not afternoon sun. Try for a location that has some wind protection. The east side of the house is a good location. Before planting, dig some organic matter into the soil. Choose a heat-resistant variety for longer bloom. Plant the seeds between mid-February and mid-March, and water them regularly. As soon as the seeds are planted, put up string or a trellis so the tender young vines are not disturbed later by an attempt to install a support. As the weather warms later in the spring, mulch the ground around the sweet peas to keep it cool. These practices should produce a good crop of sweet peas, barring a late heavy freeze or early hailstorm.

To grow cutting flowers, either annuals or perennials, that will provide bouquets all summer, select colors that will go well with the decor of the house. Determine the heights, colors, and times the plants flower. Then plan the bed as you would any other flower bed, with various colors and heights of flowers spread throughout the bed and the taller flowers in back. Select some white flowers or plants with silver foliage. Dusty miller, white statice, baby's breath, or artemisia would be good choices. Plant these between the cutting flowers to tie the whole garden together and separate colors that do not complement each other.

Several temporary shade structures can be used to provide immediate shade in a new house with very small trees. One possibility is to put up a wire or inexpensive wood trellis and grow annual vines on it, such as scarlet runner beans, heavenly blue morning glories, or even cucumbers. Large flowers can also be used for shade. Tithonia, or Mexican sunflower, giant cannas, Maximillian sunflowers, and castor beans are all good choices. The seeds and seed pods of the castor bean are quite poisonous, although the processed oil extracted from the beans is used as a laxative. If livestock or small children are in the area, do not plant castor beans. To prevent neighborhood children or animals accidentally eating the seed, cut off the seed heads as soon as they begin to develop. Some people get a skin rash when they came in contact with the leaves or seeds. The plant is large and fast-growing; it can form a hedge ten feet tall in one summer, although it will freeze in the winter. Castor bean seeds are generally not on display in garden centers, but several places have them if asked. When the soil is thoroughly warm, plant the seeds four to six feet apart, along a trench for easy watering. Castor beans are heavy water users. The leaves on young plants are quite large, sometimes as much as three feet across, while those on older plants are somewhat smaller.

Tithonia, also called Mexican sunflower, can be used as a small hedge or to shade a wall or patio. It is a large plant, with bright orange flowers, that rapidly grows to a height of six to eight feet. The leaves are rough and somewhat hairy, like sunflower leaves only smaller. The plant puts on quite a show of bright flowers from midsummer to frost. It is more drought-tolerant than castor beans.

Any annual flowering plant can be grown in a container. Select the plants so that the texture and color of the foliage as well as the flower colors go well together. Silver foliage with deep purple flowers or red and white flowers are attractive possibilities. A twelve-inch diameter pot will hold about ten plants. As many as nineteen plants can be grown in an eighteen-inch pot. Do not put more than three different species in a twelve-inch pot or more than five species in an eighteen-inch pot.

When planting in large containers use lightweight potting soil or soil-less potting mix. If the container is more than twelve inches deep, fill the bottom with Styrofoam packing beads or other lightweight material to reduce the volume of potting soil and the weight of the pot.

Water the plants well when they are planted and set the pot in a location that is out of the wind. The plants will need less water if they are placed where they do not get direct sunlight in midafternoon. Water the containers each time the top two inches of soil dry out. On hot, windy days they may need to be watered twice a day. Use a water soluble fertilizer according to the directions on the package at least once a month.

Remove spent flowers to make the plants flower longer. If plants do die before the summer is over, they can be replaced with others that will bloom in the fall. Pansies can be planted in the containers in the fall and put in a protected place for the winter, for extra early pansies for the patio the next year.

The easiest way to keep impatiens, geraniums, and some other plants over the winter is to make cuttings and bring them inside. Simply cut or break four- to six-inch pieces off the stems and put them in water. Impatiens can be grown in jars of water all winter if a dilute solution of water soluble fertilizer is added every few weeks. The cuttings can also be potted after they have formed roots. Geraniums should be potted immediately. Plant them in moist potting soil in six-inch pots. The plants can be grown inside all winter then planted outside in late spring. To make the plants bushier, pinch them back when the stems are about six inches long. Be sure to acclimate them to the outdoors gradually in the spring before setting them out.

BULBS

SPRING-FLOWERING BULBS

Spring-flowering bulbs produce roots in the fall, develop their flower buds in the winter, flower in the spring, produce and store food after they flower, then fade and lie dormant in the summer. Be sure a bulb bed is well watered in the fall. Most bulbs need soil with good drainage to keep them from rotting during their dormant periods but need plenty of water during their most-active growth stages. When the leaves first start to appear in late winter or early spring, water and apply a small amount of fertilizer. Fertilize again after flowering. Cut off the stems and flower heads of daffodils, tulips, and other spring-flowering bulbs after they bloom, but let the leaves remain on the plant until they wilt and turn brown. The leaves will continue to produce food for the bulb, which will store the food and use it to produce larger, healthier flowers next spring.

Spring-flowering bulbs should be planted between mid-September and late October. They can be planted later than that but will have smaller root systems and be less likely to survive if conditions are not just right. A good rule of thumb is to plant bulbs at a depth of three to four times their diameter. Bulbs in warmer areas can be planted more shallowly than in colder areas. Dig a hole deeper than required for planting, mix the soil in the bottom of the hole with a high phosphate fertilizer, cover the fertilizer with sand or sandy soil, then plant the bulb.

To plant a bulb border, till or dig the soil deeply and mix in some organic matter and phosphate fertilizer. Place the bulb, pointed side up, in the hole. If the soil is well prepared, a trowel can be used. Stab the soil with the trowel, pull it forward and drop the bulb in behind the trowel. Be sure the bulb goes in the hole pointed side up. Pull the trowel out and the soil will fall over the bulb. Proceed systematically from one end to the other so bulbs that are already planted are not stabbed. When all the bulbs are planted, water the bed to settle the soil.

Many types of spring-flowering bulbs are available. The most popular large bulbs are tulips, narcissus (or daffodils), and hyacinths. Popular small bulbs include crocus, snowdrops, scilla, and grape hyacinths. These are good bulbs to start with for those who are not familiar with growing bulbs.

Buy firm, healthy bulbs. Large bulbs are worth the price. Small "bargain" bulbs may not flower the first or even second spring. Study pictures and descriptions to select colors, but bear in mind that the color in photographs does not always come out exactly true. Colors of blue to purple flowers are most likely to be distorted.

Tulip bulbs can be planted until December. However, if the bulbs were stored in the refrigerator or other cool place, do not plant them until the soil temperature falls below 40°F. If they are planted earlier, they will think spring has come and start growing too soon. Monitor the soil temperature in the bulb bed with an inexpensive soil thermometer. If the bulbs were stored with apples or other ethylene-producing fruit or vegetables, they may not flower. Ethylene can prevent flowers from developing. Generally flower initiation takes from eight to ten weeks, so one or two weeks of exposure may not cause a problem, but the number of flowers may be reduced for one season.

Grape hyacinths will reseed themselves easily. They can take over large areas because they propagate themselves both by division and by seed. If only one color of grape hyacinth is in the yard, the new plants will be like the one that produced the seed. If more than one color is present, the new plants that grow from seed will produce flowers with varied colors. The color mix will depend on the genetics of each of the parent plants.

The art of planting flowers so they seem natural is called naturalizing. Bags of bulbs called a naturalizing mix are available from nurseries and garden catalogs. These bulbs are traditional varieties and are considerably less expensive than the newer hybrids. The bulbs are generally sold by the dozen. Three or four dozen bulbs will make an attractive backyard display. To look natural, the bulbs should be spaced irregularly. Gently toss handfuls of the bulbs on the ground and plant them four to six inches deep where they fall. A handful of compost can be added as each bulb is planted.

If bulbs aren't blooming they are probably too crowded. After they flower each year, if they are healthy and conditions are right, bulbs divide. Soon several bulbs are in each place where one was planted. Every few years dig up the bulbs and replant them. After they have finished flowering and the leaves are fading, dig up each clump of plants. To replant them in the same area mix about a tablespoon of fertilizer containing nitrogen and phosphate into the soil at the bottom of the hole and put a little soil on top of it. A handful of aged manure and mineral sources of phosphate can also be used. Put a layer of soil on top of the fertilized soil. Pull the bulbs apart without breaking the base and put the three largest bulbs in each hole. Planting in groups of three to five makes the planting look more natural. Or all the bulbs can be separated, tossed into the planting area, and each bulb planted where it falls. Be sure to put a little fertilizer in each planting hole but do not overdo it. If you have more bulbs than you need, start a new bed, share them with friends and neighbors, or discard them.

Getting flowers to bloom indoors before their normal bloom period is called forcing. Some varieties are easier to force than others. If the bulbs are good quality large bulbs, you should be able to force them to bloom in late winter. Bulbs need warm temperatures to develop roots, cool temperatures to initiate flower development, then warm temperature again for the leaves and flowers to grow. Put the bulbs in a pot so that just the tips are emerging from the soil. Water them well and leave them outdoors or put them in the refrigerator. Roots will begin to develop first, then flower bud initiation will begin inside the bulb. Keep them moist even after the weather gets cold. To make sure they have enough cold weather, do not bring them inside or take them out of the refrigerator until late January. When they are brought in, place them in a sunny window; they should have flowers by the end of February. For earlier flowers, buy precooled bulbs. Precooled bulbs can be planted indoors immediately and will flower in midwinter.

Many of the small bulbs will have leaves showing above the surface of the soil in the fall. Grape hyacinths should come up in September or October. The leaves of wood hyacinths, snowdrops, and scilla also come up quite early and will stay green all winter. They will photosynthesize at a slow rate through the winter but will provide some of the food the bulb needs to produce flowers in late winter. A little later, crocus leaves will begin showing. They can also tolerate below-freezing temperatures, so don't be concerned if the leaves are up and green in February or even January. Tulip and daffodil leaves should appear later. They can survive cool temperatures but not a whole winter of below-freezing temperatures. If for some reason tulips or daffodils have sprouted before February, mulch the beds with leaves or some other organic matter. They may survive the winter without harm, although in a severe winter they could freeze back completely. If the leaves do freeze during the winter, the bulbs should be strong enough to grow new leaves in early spring provided they were large, healthy bulbs.

SUMMER BULBS, TUBERS, AND CORMS

Many plants that should be dug up and stored over the winter do not have true bulbs, but they do have underground storage organs such as tubers or corms that cannot survive being frozen. Some of the most common are gladiolus, cannas, dahlias, tuberous begonias, caladium, and ranunculus. Tuberoses and gloriosa lilies should also be lifted in the fall. In the warmer parts of the region or in a warm, protected location in the central Southwest, most can be left in the ground all winter.

A Styrofoam cooler makes a good storage chest for warm-season bulbs, tubers, and corms. Put a layer of slightly damp sand in the bottom of the cooler, place a layer of bulbs, tubers, or corms upside down in the sand, and cover them with another layer of sand. Make sure the sand is only slightly damp, not wet, or the plant parts will rot. Do not allow them to touch each other. Continue layering, with all the plant parts placed upside down in the sand until they are all in the cooler. Take the cooler to a garage or other storage area with cool but not freezing temperatures. When the cooler is in place, place a cup of water in the container. The water will evaporate gradually and keep the corms and tubers from shriveling. Check them at least once a month. Add more water if the cup is empty and remove any parts that are drying or rotting.

Begonias

Begonia tubers should be planted with the concave or depressed side up. The sprouts come from the center of that depressed side. They can be started indoors in a warm, light spot in late winter but should not be put outdoors until late May. When they are put outdoors, they require a moist, shady site. They work well on the north or east side of the house. Water the begonias regularly, but avoid getting water on the leaves in late afternoon, as wet leaves at night can promote disease. Pick off all the dead flowers to prolong blooming until frost. Before frost, take the plants inside, withhold water until the leaves wilt, then cut them off. The tubers can be left in the pot all winter or stored as described above. If they are left in the pot, be careful not to overwater them when they are not growing.

Dahlias

Dahlias can be propagated from seed, division of tubers, or cuttings. To produce several plants from one tuber, plant the tubers in pots in mid-winter and keep them indoors. When the sprouts are about six inches tall, cut off the top four inches of each growing tip. Dip the base of the cuttings in rooting hormone and root them in a flat of moist potting soil. They will be ready to set out by early summer. When the tubers have put on another six inches of growth, make another set of cuttings. Up to a dozen plants can be produced from each tuber.

Daylilies

Like many other perennials, daylilies should be divided every three or four years. Daylilies can be divided just about any time, but the best time is after they finish blooming in the summer or early fall. To divide them, dig up the clump, separate the plants, and replant the healthiest ones. Dividing a clump of daylilies may be difficult. Pry them apart with a pair of garden forks or cut the clump with a large sharp knife or shovel. Each replanted plant should have a cluster of healthy looking leaves and several plump, small tubers on the roots. Plant them so the crown, or the point where the roots meet the leaves, is at the surface of the soil. After mid-October the roots will not have much time to reestablish themselves before the soil freezes in colder areas. Be sure to mulch them to keep the plants from being ripped from the soil as a result of freezing and thawing.

Glads

Wait until at least mid-April to plant the first glad corms. After that plant a few each week to extend the bloom period. If they are all planted the same week, they will all flower at about the same time. By extending the planting period from April through early July, you will have flowers all summer and into the fall.

If the glads are dug at the end of the summer there may be little growths around the base of the corm. The little growths are called cormels, and if they are planted next year, they will grow into little gladioli plants. It will take about three years before they are big enough to produce flowers.

Irises

Iris rhizomes multiply each year and need to be divided every three or four years. To divide the plants, first cut the foliage back to about four inches. Then dig up the entire clump. Shake off the soil and examine the clump. Cut off the largest, healthiest rhizomes, making sure each section has some roots and a bit of foliage. Mix some bulb fertilizer or superphosphate into the soil and put the large healthy rhizomes back into the soil, planting them just below the surface, about a foot apart. Discard any rhizomes that look diseased or are especially small. If you have more healthy rhizomes than needed, give them away to other gardeners.

Mosaic virus can cause yellow streaking in leaves and color breaks in iris flowers. It can be spread by aphids as they go from one plant to the next, or by scissors or clippers. If an infected plant is cut, sterilize the scissors or clippers in a chlorine bleach solution before cutting an uninfected plant. Mosaic virus is not a common problem. Different strains of virus produce similar symptoms on roses, vegetables, and many other plants. There is no cure. To eliminate the virus, remove the infected plants and destroy them. The virus will not stay in the soil once the plants are removed. To avoid reinfecting your garden, buy new plants only from reliable sources.

Easter lilies

Easter lilies can be planted outside. They should be planted in a rich, well-drained soil. Mix some organic matter with the soil to a depth of about eighteen inches. Remove the lily from the pot and plant it so the top of the bulb is six inches below the surface of the soil. Place a stake next to the bulb when it is planted so the stalk can be tied up in the spring without piercing the bulb. The lily will not flower again the year it is planted; the next year it will come up in early spring and should be flowering by early summer. It will be taller than it was in the pot because the size of lilies is carefully controlled in greenhouse production for Easter. When allowed to grow naturally, Easter lilies can be four to six feet tall.

PERENNIALS

A perennial bed takes less care than an annual bed and can be attractive for many years once it is established. Iris and daylilies can be used to fill in a flowerless period in May or June between spring bulbs and summer flowers. Look for late-season iris and early-season daylilies for easy-care plants to fill in that period. Peonies, columbines, and dianthus also bloom in May or June. Geraniums can be set out in the perennial bed if it is in bright sunlight. New varieties of geraniums are available in almost every shade of white, pink, and red. With some planning, flowers can be blooming in the perennial bed all but two or three months out of the year.

The type of carnation florists grow from seed is easy to propagate. Several garden centers in the area also sell them as bedding plants. If grown from seed, they should be started in late winter so they will be ready to set out in midspring. Producing the quality of carnation florists generate in the greenhouse is more difficult. To produce large, high-quality carnations, start by supporting the stems so they grow straight and tall. Two squares of chicken wire or fence wire held six inches and twelve inches above the plant will provide the support it needs. As the stems start to produce flower buds, all but the large central bud must be removed. The earlier the side buds are removed, the larger the central flower will be. If fertilized and watered well, the carnations can grow as large as the florist's.

Chrysanthemums are classed by the number of weeks it takes them to flower after the days start getting shorter. A greenhouse variety mum that takes several weeks of short days to bloom will survive outside and grow into a large bushy plant each summer. But it will only flower when the weather stays warm long enough for the flower buds to develop and open, which will not be every year. Chrysanthemums are called hardy when the roots are hardy. The blossoms cannot withstand freezing weather. If the plant is in a protected place and is covered when frost is predicted, the buds may open. Cold weather frequently causes some discoloration of the flowers, however.

Getting peonies to grow in the Southwest can be difficult. Peonies should be planted in the sun but their roots should be mulched or shaded. They will also fail to bloom if they are planted too deep. The buds should be just below the surface of the soil. Fertilize them in early summer, to make sure the roots are strong and healthy. When peonies are planted properly, they should not be dug for several years.

VARIETIES

For shady areas of the garden, try the new impatiens varieties. Several dwarf or compact varieties are available, including Bright Eye and the Super Elfin series. Show Stopper impatiens have a cascading habit that makes them good for hanging baskets and containers, and there are several new two-toned releases. The Spectra series of New Guinea impatiens flowers best with some sunlight. Several new pastel shades, including bluish and lavender, look particularly refreshing when they bloom on hot summer days.

Encore begonias will also provide all-summer bloom in the shade. Green- and bronze-leafed varieties flower in shades of pink, red, and white. Illumination begonia is a hybrid that produces large double pink flowers, some of which have cream-color centers.

Flowers that can grow in partial shade or sun include canna, columbine, delphinium, and alyssum. Zebra Sunset is a new variegated canna that can tolerate more sun than many other variegated cannas. A new series of columbines called the Songbird series bears large flowers in shades of blue, pink, and white. The plants grow from eighteen to thirty inches in height. Southern Nobleman delphiniums are good cutting flowers. They have long, strong stems and come in various shades of blue, purple, burgundy, plum, white, and bicolors. Another new delphinium is Sungleam. It has creamy yellow flowers and can grow to be six feet tall. Delphiniums tend to live for only a few years in the Southwest. Pastel Carpet alyssum comes in shades of pink, lilac, white, yellow, rose, and purple. This is an old favorite that is even better due to recent improvements.

Some new drought-tolerant plants have also been released in the past several years. These include Yellow Sun gaillardia, a dwarf annual that forms a fourteen-inch mound covered with two-inch ball-shape yellow blooms. Silver Brocade artemisia is a perennial that grows to six inches tall and spreads thirty inches. It has deeply lobed, soft, velvety silver foliage. An old lavender that has not always been available in the United States is Alba, a white form of English lavender. Dainty Blue lavender grows to eighteen inches and has fragrant flowers on slender stalks. Blue Lisa and Hallelujah Hybrids are new lisianthus hybrids that will thrive in full sun. Blue Lisa is a deep blue dwarf variety. Hallelujah Hybrids grow to twenty-four inches and have bicolor flowers that are three inches in diameter.

Many of these varieties are released through wholesale distributors and are available in local nurseries. Others are available through Thompson and Morgan, Liberty Seed Co., White Flower Farm, and other nursery catalogs.

Some mail order companies are quite reputable and have good quality plants. Many rare plants may be available only through a catalog. Companies that offer mature, good quality plants generally have competitive prices and only rarely offer special sales. Companies that regularly advertise extremely low prices either offer plant material of lower quality or material that is less mature. Obviously if nurseries can cut a year or two off the production time of their products, they can sell them for less. They may, for example, offer a very low price on tulip bulbs, but when the bulbs arrive, they are all less than an inch in diameter and will not produce flowers the following spring.

An important consideration in purchasing plants through the mail is their adaptation to our southwestern climate. In order to assure that plants are adapted to local conditions, make major landscape purchases from local nurseries with trained personnel.

SHADE GARDENS

Most naturally shady situations have acid soils because they are in the shade of trees that drop their leaves, producing large quantities of humic acid in the soil. Since our soil is quite alkaline, the number of shade plants we can grow is limited.

Annuals and biennials that will grow in the shade here include begonias, which will survive if they are moved indoors during the winter, impatiens, browallia, coleus, and some campanulas. These need to be replanted each year. Perennials that will flower in the shade include aegopodium, ajuga, anemone, bergenia, bleeding heart, foxglove, lilies, liriope, lily of the valley, phlox, vinca, violets, and columbine, although powdery mildew is a problem with columbines in the shade. Some of these can be invasive. Few flowering shrubs will grow in the shade or tolerate our alkaline soil. Mahonia and some viburnums will grow in light shade. *Kerria japonica* can tolerate somewhat deeper shade. Of these, all must be irrigated, but browallia, ajuga, aegopodium, liriope, phlox, vinca, violets, and mahonia can tolerate the least water. Bush morning glory, native cranesbills, and yellow columbine will survive in light shade and require very little water.

More choices are available for the northeast side of the house, where the plants will get some sun, than directly north of the house. Some flowering plants to try on the northeast side are begonias, foxglove, impatiens, sweet alyssum, nicotiana, salvia, vinca minor, columbines, violets, grape hyacinth, and daylily. Colorful foliage plants include coleus, hosta, goutweed, ajuga, and blue fescue ornamental grass. Most of these plants require moist, well-drained soil, so add plenty of organic matter to the soil before planting, then water well. Leave at least eighteen inches between the plants and the house. This helps prevent damage to the foundation and walls from roots and water.

Cuttings from houseplants can be used to fill in temporary bare spots in a border, especially in the shade. Coleus, purple velvet plant, or other plants with colorful leaves are particularly attractive in a flowering border. Philodendron, Swedish ivy, English ivy, and pothos also root easily. Take the cuttings, root them indoors in a rooting medium or fine potting soil, then acclimate them to the outdoors gradually over a period of a couple of weeks. Keep them well watered when they are first set out, then gradually reduce the water to a normal watering schedule. Many houseplants will spread for the rest of the summer and fill in the space very nicely until the first frost.

SPECIALTY GARDENS

Before trying to attract butterflies to the garden, remember that butterflies are insects. They are the mature forms of caterpillars. Therefore, do not use insecticides in a garden designed to attract butterflies.

A number of plants will attract butterflies to the garden. Bee balm, coreopsis, wild indigo, goldenrod, Queen Anne's lace, butterfly weed, sweet alyssum, and common milkweed are some of them. Try to have flowers blooming in all seasons to provide nectar for the butterflies, and grow plants like milkweed, parsley, clover, asters, marigolds, and morning glories for the larvae. As a rule, butterflies have little interest in double flowers or in gladioli, peonies, or roses. Some butterflies prefer, at various stages in their life cycle, things like fresh manure, mud puddles, or carrion. It may be best to try to attract butterflies that share your taste in plants, and to attempt to attract them in a moderate way to limit the number of caterpillars in the garden.

For a low-water-use butterfly garden start with a foundation of a few shrubs. Indigo bush, autumn sage, potentilla, and a few hardy, old-fashioned shrub roses will make a good foundation for the garden. They will need some supplemental water to keep them flowering, but they all attract butterflies. Other easy-to-grow plants that are somewhat drought tolerant but need supplemental water include butterfly weed, monarda (or bee balm), black-eyed Susans, orange mountain daisies, and showy milkweed. Coreopsis, gayfeather, and gaillardia use even less water, and coneflowers and desert marigold can grow and flower without supplemental water once they are established.

To attract as many butterflies as possible, use plants that flower over a long period of time. Monarda, potentilla, and orange mountain daisies flower in the spring. Potentilla and monarda will continue to flower into the summer when the butterfly weed, indigo bush, black-eyed Susans, coreopsis, gaillardia, and desert marigold will also start flowering. Many of the summer-flowering plants will continue to flower until frost. Gayfeather and autumn sage will round out the fall flowers in the garden.

To supplement the flowers with some caterpillar food, plant dill, mint, catnip, and other herbs near the plants that need supplemental water. Other members of the mint family or daisy family can complete the butterfly garden.

A low-water-use garden can provide color for the entire growing season. For early spring flowers, start with species tulips and other bulbs. California poppy, blue or scarlet flax, iris, pinks, coreopsis, gaillardia, Rocky Mountain penstemon, black-eyed Susan, coneflower, baby's breath, gayfeather, and chocolate flower will give a long season of color.

Most of these flowers come in shades of yellow, orange, or purple, creating a striking display of color. They have long blooming seasons and are easy for the beginner to grow. Most of them are readily available at nurseries, either as bedding plants or seeds.

To create a rock garden from a naturally rocky slope start with a few accent shrubs, like cliff rose, apache plume, threeleaf or little-leaf sumac, or mountain mahogany. Place these just above large boulders. They grow this way naturally because the boulders stop water and debris from running down the slope, so the soil is wetter and richer there. Scatter a few smaller shrubs among the boulders. Dalea, artemisia, or creeping sumac are good choices. Add some yucca or ornamental grasses for contrasting shapes and textures. Finally work in some flowers like penstemon, gayfeather, California poppy, coneflower, blue flax, and evening primrose for color and some ground covers like snow-in-summer or sedum to cover the remaining bare spots.

Butterfly Garden Plants

Bee balm
Coreopsis
Wild indigo
Goldenrod
Queen Annes Lace
Butterfly weed
Sweet alyssum
Common Indigo bush
Autumn sage
Potentilla
Hardy, old fashioned shrub roses
Butterfly weed
Monarda, or bee balm
Black-eyed Susans
Orange mountain daisies
Showy milkweed
Coreopsis
Gayfeather
Gaillardia
Coneflowers
Desert marigold
Autumn sage

CATERPILLAR FOOD

Dill
Mint
Catnip
Milkweed
Parsley
Clover
Asters
Marigolds
Morning glories
Other members of the mint family or daisy family

Irrigation will be needed to establish the plants, and some of the plants listed above will need continued supplemental irrigation. Install a drip system to give the plants the water they need and cover it with mulch to protect the plastic from deterioration in the sun.

Water gardens are becoming increasingly popular. Water gardens can be anything from a large pot filled with water and a few aquatic plants to a carefully constructed pond. Hardy water lilies and fish can spend the winter in a pond. Clean the pond in fall to minimize the accumulation of gasses that are released as organic matter rots. Remove the goldfish or koi from the pond and put them in a tank. Drain the pond and remove all decaying organic matter. Trim the leaves of the water lilies and place their pots on the bottom of the pond. Refill the pond and dechlorinate the water. Return the fish to the pond as soon as the temperature of the water in the pond is the same as the temperature in the tank.

The fish can adapt to living in an ice-covered pond, but they still need oxygen. In high elevation areas, a portable cold frame over the pond can keep the pond from freezing over. Make a frame large enough to cover the pond. (If it is a large pond, it may be easier to cover only a section.) Use a two-by-twelve for the north end of the frame and a two-by-six for the south end so the covering will slope slightly and snow and rain can run off. Form the sides with one-by-twelves cut to an appropriate slope and braced by two-by-fours. Add two-by-four braces as necessary to keep the frame rigid over the pond. Cover the entire frame with fiberglass. Make a small door in the material so you can check to see if the pond is ice covered in cold weather and ventilate it on warm sunny days.

DRIED FLOWERS

Many plants make attractive dried arrangements. Some are common garden flowers; others are native to the Southwest. Gayfeather, winterfat, santolina, and Indian ricegrass are good natives to plant, either for dried flowers or seed heads to add to arrangements. Yarrow, cockscomb, statice, baby's breath, winged everlasting, Xeranthemum, strawflower, and many ornamental grasses are easily cultivated in the Southwest and make attractive dried arrangements. Other flowers can be dried effectively under the right conditions, although colors frequently fade when the flowers are dried.

Start by collecting about twice the volume of plant material that will be needed. Collect only material that is in the best condition. Plant materials may be dried in three ways. The first is air drying. Simply tie the material together in small bunches and hang it upside down to dry. Strip foliage from plant stems before drying as foliage frequently turns brown and unattractive even when the flower retains its color. Flowers that air dry easily include strawflower, globe amaranth, baby's breath, gayfeather, goldenrod, grains and grasses, larkspur, rose, tansy, and yarrow.

A second way to dry flowers is to cover them with a dry mixture of two-thirds borax and one-third sand. Silica gel and cornmeal can also be used in the same proportions. Place some of the material in the bottom of a box. Place the flowers upside down on the material and gently sift more of the material over them. Stems may need to be removed and replaced with wire before drying flowers by this method. Place the box in a cool, dry place for two weeks, then gently remove the flowers from the mixture and brush them off with a small, soft paintbrush. Plants that dry well by this method include bleeding heart, candytuft, daisy, delphinium, gloxinia, lilac, lily of the valley, marigold, pansy, snapdragon, chrysanthemum, stocks, violet, rose, and zinnia.

The third way to preserve foliage is to place the stems in a mixture of one-third glycerin and two-thirds water. The glycerin is absorbed by the plant leaves and preserves them without allowing them to become dry and brittle. Barberry, canna leaves, euonymus, ivy, Russian olive, silver leaf poplar, and rubber plant can be preserved this way. Cannas, rubber plants, and other large-leafed plants require a 50 percent glycerin solution, and some of the leaves will be more attractive when preserved if they are soaked in the solution. This is also true of ivy and rubber plant.

Homegrown lavender can be used to make sweet-smelling sachets. Pick the flower spikes when they are not quite fully open, leaving enough stem on each spike so they can be tied together. Tie a ribbon or string around each handful and hang it upside down to dry. The bunches can be hung in closets as they are, or the flowers can be stripped and mixed with other flowers and herbs to make a potpourri. The potpourri can then be wrapped in cheesecloth, netting, or other loose-weave cloth for sachets. Some people like the smell of lavender and sage; others prefer a more subtle scent of roses or violets with lavender. Oils and extracts can be purchased to supplement the natural scents. The low humidity in the Southwest is excellent for drying flowers and plants, but scents are not released as well nor do they travel as far on dry air as they do on more humid air. Lavender sachets used in New Mexico will be more subtle than those in more humid places.

CHAPTER 8

Roses

Before going to buy roses, have a plan for the garden and some idea of the size and color you want. Nursery staff will be able to suggest varieties that fit those plans. Examine individual plants to be sure the roots are plump and healthy. Darkened or shriveled spots on the roots indicate a problem. Examine the crown, where the stem meets the roots. It will have a grafting scar and perhaps a slight difference in size between the root-stock and top part of the plant, but there should be no pronounced swelling or knobs at that point. The bark on the stem should be firm, without any dark spots or shriveling. The buds should be plump and healthy looking but not expanded. If the leaves of a bare-root rose start growing before it is planted, the food reserves of the plant will be used up, and the roots will not get a good start when it is planted. Plant a rose with expanding leaves in a pot indoors until established roses start to leaf out. It might freeze if planted outside too early. Containerized roses can be planted later in the year with leaves fully expanded.

The graft should be just at the soil surface, the planting hole should be big enough to accommodate all the roots, and the rose should be protected until the weather is warm and the rose has started to grow. For best results improve all the soil in the rose bed rather than just amending the soil used to backfill the hole after planting.

Most roses can tolerate cold weather and even some frost without damage. Cut back on water in fall to protect roses in winter. This will cause them to grow more slowly and be a little tougher when winter comes. Do not give them any fertilizer after midsummer and don't prune them, even lightly.

After the leaves fall off, mound soil, tree leaves, or other organic material around the base of the plant. Bring the soil in from another location; do not dig it from the base of the plant. Different roses have different sensitivities to cold. Some roses can come through the average winter in most of the Southwest with no damage at all. Others have to be protected beginning in early winter. New or replacement plants should be mounded or covered with rose caps if they are still small.

Rose trees are hybrid roses grafted onto a stiff, upright stem. In some climates tree roses are partially dug up, laid on their sides, and covered with insulating mulch or soil each winter. In other areas they are not hardy outside at all and must be put in a container and brought inside for the winter. Fortunately we do not have to go to such extremes to protect them here. Most species of tree roses will survive without any protection at all, if the weather cools off gradually so the roses have a chance to acclimatize to colder weather. One way to protect a tree rose in the colder parts of the region is to build a wire cage around it and fill the cage with leaves or crumpled newspaper. Another way is to wrap the plant in newspapers. Use several layers and hold them in place by spiraling twine around them and tying. The area around the graft needs the most protection, so wrap that very well. Do not wrap just the graft, however, because the extra weight of the wrapping may cause the top of the plant to break off in strong winds.

Roses should be pruned just as their buds start to swell in the spring. Start examining the buds in late February to determine if they have started to expand. Prune them when they begin to expand, usually in March or April.

To prune the roses, start by cutting off anything that is dead and any sprouts that come from below the graft or from the roots. If a cane is dead it will have shriveled bark or will be a gray color, and the smaller twigs will snap easily. A dead cane will have no expanding buds. Climbing roses do not need any further pruning at this time. Floribundas and grandifloras should be cut back and thinned to keep them a reasonable size. Remove the weaker of two canes that cross, canes growing toward the center of the bush, and some of the older canes. Cut the longer canes back by as much as a third of their length.

Hybrid tea roses are the most popular and require the most pruning. After cutting out anything that is dead, diseased, or damaged, select three to five healthy young canes that are spaced so as to form a bowl. Remove other canes. Cut the selected canes back to twenty-four inches on moderately vigorous plants. On extremely vigorous plants that have room to grow, cut the plant to twenty-four to thirty-six inches. For exhibition roses, cut the canes to six to ten inches. Remove lateral branches and small twigs.

Shrub roses generally need very little pruning compared to hybrid tea roses. Young plants may not need to be pruned at all. Remove any dead wood. If the plants are taller than appropriate for the space, cut back the

---

Easy Care Roses

Shrub

Bonica

Simplicity

Miedland varieties

Climbers

Improved Blaze

Climbing Peace

Climbing Double Delight

Floribunda

Europeana

Hybrid tea and Grandiflora

Peace

Mr. Lincoln

Queen Elizabeth

Tournament of Roses

Honor

Almost all species and old fashioned roses.

taller stems. Make each cut just above an outward-facing bud. As the shrubs get older, remove some older stems in early spring. Some new shrub roses bloom all summer. Remove the old flowers from the rose to improve its appearance and assure new flowers for as long as possible.

If the bush was pruned properly in the spring, the only pruning the rosebush will need in summer is the removal of blossoms. After a stem has finished blooming, look down the stem and find the first leaf with five leaflets. If it faces outward, cut the cane about a quarter-inch above the leaf. If it faces toward the center of the bush, follow the stem to the first outward-facing leaf and cut above that leaf.

Light fertilization will help the roses. Put about a tablespoon of a balanced fertilizer under each bush in midspring and again in early summer. Spread the fertilizer under the entire bush and scratch it into the soil lightly, then water the shrub.

Many climbing roses flower only on old wood, so pruning all the canes back every year will prevent them from flowering. Cut out a few of the old canes each year and cut back the new canes to fit the space available, but do not cut them all the way back like hybrid tea roses. Climbing roses should be pruned after the first flush of flowers in the summer. Climbing roses are also more likely to flower if they are trained horizontally rather then vertically. Tie the canes to a support so they form an arch.

Roses should not be pruned in fall unless they have extremely long canes. Winter weather may damage the tips of branches, but these can easily be trimmed off. However, canes that are allowed to blow in the wind may be damaged close to the crown, which weakens the plant. Cut long canes back in late summer but do not cut them as far back as for spring pruning.

Roses can be propagated from cuttings. The wood of the cuttings should still be supple and young. Take rose cuttings in summer just after the petals have dropped. Count down six sets of leaves from the top and cut off the stem. Remove the two bottom sets of leaves. Cut off the top two

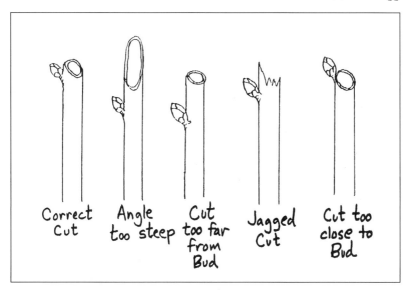

Correct Cut | Angle too steep | Cut too far from Bud | Jagged Cut | Cut too close to Bud

sets of leaves by cutting the stem at an angle just below the second leaf. Dip the base in rooting hormone powder and put it into a prepared cutting bed. Be sure to take several cuttings as all of them will not root successfully. Put a jar over each cutting and cover each jar with a white paper bag to prevent burning or overheating. Keep the rooting bed moist. Small new leaves will appear in a few weeks but don't disturb the cutting or jar until spring. Then transplant the young plants to the rose garden. Many new rose varieties are protected by plant patent and should not be propagated by cuttings.

To prepare the cutting bed, select a site that is in the sun for at least six hours a day but preferably not in the late afternoon. Loosen the soil and mix in some compost to help hold water. For poor soil, add some phosphate fertilizer but do not add nitrogen. Nitrogen fertilizer can easily burn off tender new roots. Level the soil and pat it by hand; don't stamp it down or pack the soil.

Although we have fewer problems with roses than gardeners in more humid areas, some roses are harder to grow than others. Hybrid tea roses generally take a lot of care, but rugosa roses can be almost ignored and still flower all summer. They are seldom bothered by mildew or insects. They bloom first thing in the spring and keep flowering until frost. Spent flowers do not have to be removed. Most varieties have large, bright red rose hips, or fruit, that follow the flowers. The rose hips can be harvested and made into a flavorful jelly. Rugosa rose flowers are very fragrant.

Two highly recommended rugosa roses are Henry Hudson, a semi-double white that makes a rounded shrub, and Martin Frobisher, a semi-double pink that makes a very upright, bushy shrub. These two will have to be ordered from catalogs but others are available locally. A recent renewed interest in hardier types of roses has brought old-fashioned roses back on the market.

Several varieties of new hybrid shrub roses originally developed at the House of Meidiland are now being sold quite widely. They have a profuse show of double flowers and are more disease resistant and cold hardy than hybrid tea or floribunda roses. Their flowers are generally smaller and are shaped more like old-fashioned roses than hybrid teas. The flowers on some of the varieties, however, are three to four inches across.

The shrubs come in a variety of shapes and sizes and can be used as ground covers or accent shrubs. They require only minimal pruning if they require pruning at all. They will make a loose, informal hedge and can be used as barrier plantings.

CHAPTER 9

Vegetables and Herbs

PLANNING

Winter is the time to begin planning for vegetable gardens. Individuals who have never had a vegetable garden before, should start by putting a plan down on paper.

Figure out how large a space is available for vegetables. Outline the space on a piece of paper, including all nearby walls or trees. Use graph paper to make the drawing to scale.

Decide between the intensive method or planting in rows. If the space is small, the intensive method is better. Plants are planted in a block with equal spacing on all sides. The space between plants in each direction is the number of inches listed on the seed packet for space between plants in the row.

The number of plants you need will depend on whether you plan to can or freeze some of the produce. For example, two or three tomato plants will provide all the fresh tomatoes a family will need, but twenty plants will be necessary to provide the average person with all the processed tomatoes, sauce, juice, and ketchup they will use in a year. Make a list of your family's favorite vegetables. Plant only a few plants of a new vegetable or one your family may not like. If it turns out to be popular, you can plant more the next year.

On the average, 40 snap bean plants, 60 carrots, 50 sweet corn plants, 1 cucumber plant, 1 cantaloupe plant, 25 onions, 8 to 10 bell peppers,

50 heads of lettuce planted at different times, and about 60 radishes will provide the amounts of those fresh vegetables one person will eat. One summer squash plant will supply enough for two people if the squash bugs don't get it. These are averages, and if the family really enjoys a certain vegetable, they could eat several times that much. It is usually unrealistic to expect to produce sweet corn, watermelons, or all the lettuce the family will eat on a city lot. Plan on growing some leaf lettuce and other greens to supplement salads but to continue buying head lettuce if your family eats salads regularly. Cantaloupes, squash, and cucumbers take up a lot of space, but new bush varieties are suitable for smaller areas. Be sure all the plants will fit in the space available.

Check the catalog to determine when to plant each variety. If planting should occur as soon as the soil can be worked, plant in February or March in Albuquerque. Cool-season crops such as beets, carrots, and cabbage can be planted in late March or April, but wait to plant the warm-season crops such as cucumbers, tomatoes, and peppers. They cannot tolerate frost. The average last-frost date varies depending on altitude and local conditions. April 20 is the average date of the last frost in Albuquerque. If planted on this date, the warm-season crops have a 50–50 chance of surviving. For better odds, wait a few weeks before planting warm-season crops. In the mountains or in areas where cold air settles the last-frost date is several weeks behind the warmer areas. By late May, warm-season crops may safely be planted throughout most of the Southwest.

Many plants, such as broccoli and cabbage, do better as a fall crop than as a spring crop in the Southwest. Fall crops should be planted in July or August. Determine the number of days it takes the crop to mature from seed, then plant it that many days before October 20.

To save space and reduce the labor of preparing the soil, use succession planting. Lettuce is planted early and does not stay in the ground all summer. After all the lettuce is harvested, plant broccoli or some other fall crop in the same space. Think of the garden as three different gardens, one for spring, one for summer, and one for fall. Draw a picture of what will be in the garden in each season. For additional help in planning and caring for the garden, request the publication "Home Vegetable Gardening in New Mexico" from the Cooperative Extension Service in your county.

Soil temperature is the most important factor in seed germination. Some seeds will germinate when the soil is 40°F; for others the soil should be 60°F. Generally, the warmer the soil, the shorter the length of time for seeds to germinate. For example, lettuce will germinate in fifteen days if the soil temperature is 41°F and in two days if it is 77°F. Above 77°F, it takes longer, and at 95°F there is no germination. Most cool-season crops can be planted when the soil temperature is 50°F. Warm-season crops will come up sooner if the soil is above 70°F. The real trick is to wait long enough for the soil to warm up but not so long that the season is too short to produce a crop.

If the soil is too cold when seeds are planted, they may germinate but the resulting plants will be weak. Invest in an inexpensive soil

Optimum Germination Temperatures

Beans	60–80°F
Beets	40–90°F
Cabbage	50–70°F
Carrots	50–85°F
Corn	60–95°F
Cucumbers	60–95°F
Eggplant	75–95°F
Lettuce	32–75°F
Muskmelon	75–95°F
Onions	32–85°F
Parsley	50–75°F
Peas	40–75°F
Peppers	60–85°F
Radishes	50–85°F
Spinach	32–60°F
Tomatoes	50–90°F

thermometer and start planting when the soil temperature reaches 50°F. Because our spring weather is so variable, a soil thermometer is a much more accurate way to determine planting times than the calendar.

A vegetable garden needs fertile soil. A level area with loam soil, which is halfway between sand and clay in texture, would be a good site for a garden. If the soil is relatively uniform in texture, put the garden where it will be easy to water and will get six hours or more of direct sunlight each day. It should be a reasonably level spot and convenient to the house, to encourage daily watering, weeding, or harvesting. As soon as the site for the garden is selected, begin preparing the soil by sheet composting. Spread up to two feet of spoiled hay, manure, fresh cut weeds (without seeds), leaves, and other organic matter over the entire garden area. Water every time the material dries out and by spring the soil will be greatly improved.

Collecting old varieties of food plants has generated a great deal of interest in recent years. Some people want them for historic interest; others are trying to preserve the diversity of the genes available for breeding. In the fourteenth century the gardens of what is now New Mexico contained many varieties of corn, beans, and squash, along with some other plants grown for food, medicine, or flavoring. Several of these plants are available from Native Seeds/SEARCH in Tucson, Arizona; Plants of the Southwest in Albuquerque and Santa Fe; Seeds of Change in Gila, New Mexico; and Talavaya in Santa Cruz, New Mexico. The only records we have of these gardens are in the oral traditions of the Native Americans and the conjecture of anthropologists.

When the Spaniards arrived, they began introducing some new species, but the gardens were still used primarily for food. Those seeds are also available from the sources listed above. A few descriptions of these gardens exist in letters and reports sent to Spain by priests and soldiers. Their main interests were not gardening so the descriptions are generally sketchy.

SEEDS

Different types of seed can be kept for different lengths of time. Onion seeds, for example, remain viable for less than a year under most conditions, whereas lettuce seeds can be stored up to six years in a cool, dry location and still be viable. To test seeds, moisten a paper towel and spread five of the seeds on the towel. Fold the damp paper towel in half over the seeds, then roll it up. To keep it damp, place it on end in a jar or glass that has a small amount of water in it. Replace the water as necessary to keep the towel moist. Be sure to label each rolled towel with the names of the seeds that are inside. After three days, unroll the towels and check to see how many of the seeds have sprouted. If they have not all sprouted, roll the towel back up, return it to the jar or glass, and check it in two more days. After that, check every other day for two weeks. If fewer than three of the seeds have sprouted after two weeks, discard that packet of seeds.

BEDDING PLANTS

Healthy bedding plants are short, stocky, dark green, and have been properly hardened off, or prepared for planting outside. Cabbages that have been properly hardened off will have a whitish tint on the leaves. Some tomato varieties will have a little bit of purple on the stems. However, purple on the stems can also be a sign of disease or nutrient deficiencies. Look for other signs that the plants are healthy before purchasing them. Bedding plants should have thick stems with leaves close together along the stems. The plants should be able to stand up by themselves rather than having to lean on each other for support. A few roots growing out of the bottom of the container indicate a vigorously growing plant. However, a big tangle of roots indicates the plants have been in those containers too long. Do not buy them. Inspect the plants for insects, disease, or unusual-looking growth. If you find any of those things, don't buy the

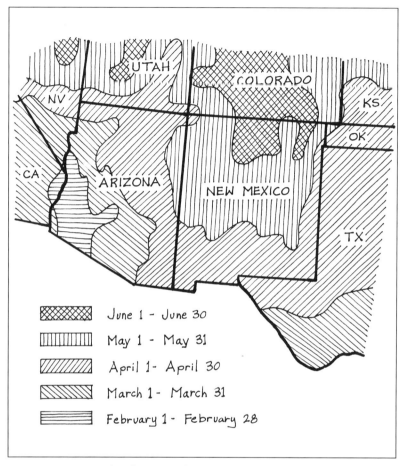

Average last-frost date for the Southwest in the spring

plant, but be sure to mention it to the nursery so they can save the part of the crop that is not yet infected. I have seen fewer insect and disease problems on bedding plants in New Mexico than I have in other states, but it still pays to examine plants before purchasing them.

The most common bedding plants started at home require a warm soil and cannot withstand frost. This group includes tomatoes and peppers.

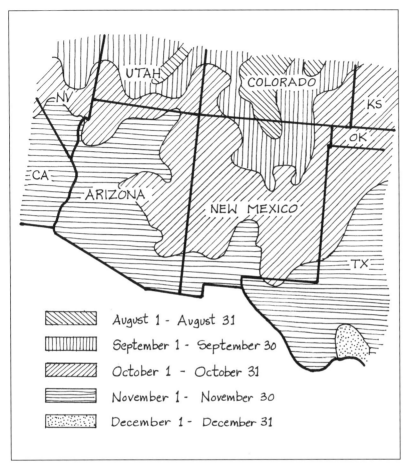

Average first-frost date for the Southwest in the fall

Start seeds of these plants indoors around the first of April. Plants should be set out a few weeks after the average last-frost date. See the map on page 162 for last-frost dates.

Another group of plants frequently started indoors are cool-season plants like broccoli, cabbage, and cauliflower. For spring planting they should be started in mid-February.

In general, large seeded plants like beans, peas, cucumbers, and melons should not be started indoors unless they are started only a couple of weeks before they should be set out and are planted in peat pots so they do not have to be transplanted. While many seeds germinate best at temperatures around 70°F, the strongest bedding plants are those that are grown at 60°F or cooler.

Most seedlings should be transplanted when they have one or two sets of true leaves because they will have smaller root systems and it will be easier to move them without destroying the roots. Fill pots with slightly damp—neither dry nor soggy—potting soil. When the pots are prepared, loosen the soil around the seedlings by slipping a plant marker or pencil under them and lifting gently. One at a time grasp each seedling by the leaves and pull it out of the loose soil. Handle the plant by the leaves rather than the stem. If the leaves are slightly damaged the plant can usually grow new ones. If the stem is damaged the plant dies. Make a hole in the soil with your finger or a pencil and place the roots of the plant into the hole. Plant the seedling at the same depth as in the seeding media. Make sure no roots are sticking out above the surface. Gently press the soil around the roots, then transplant the next seedling. With practice this procedure can be done rapidly.

After all the seedlings have been transplanted, water the pots carefully so as not to wash the seedlings out and put them in a bright, sunny place. Keep the plants slightly cooler than the seedling trays to prevent the plants from getting tall and spindly.

MULCH

After vegetables are planted, mulch the garden with three to four inches of organic matter. Use grass clippings, leaves, composted kitchen garbage, spoiled hay, or any other easily obtainable organic matter. This will keep the surface of the soil moist and add some organic matter to help prevent crusting and to improve the texture of the soil. Mulching also keeps the soil cooler and conserves water. At the end of the season, till or dig the organic matter into the soil, then add more organic matter in the spring before planting the vegetables.

GRAYWATER

Broadly defined, graywater is any waste water that doesn't go down the toilet. Graywater can be water from the shower or bath, dishwasher, washing machine, or sinks. Graywater piping systems are illegal in some cities because of potential dangers. A graywater system connected to a system that also pipes freshwater may allow graywater to be siphoned back into the freshwater system. An open system or antisiphon device can eliminate this problem.

Graywater may create problems for plants. For example, sodium, bleach, or borax can damage plants. Water softeners to which salt is added replace the calcium in the water with sodium. Softened water should not be used on plants. Dishwasher detergents generally contain compounds that could be damaging. Laundry water will contain any compounds that were on the clothes. If clothes with grease, motor oil, gasoline, diesel fuel, or pesticides were washed in the water, it should not be used to water plants. Biodegradable soaps and detergents break down into substances that act as fertilizers, but too much fertilizer can damage plants. Graywater that contains only safe, biodegradable products can be used on edible plants. If there is the chance the graywater might contain even small amounts of damaging products, use the water only on landscape plants.

FALL GARDEN

Several vegetables can be planted outside after mid-July and still be expected to produce before they freeze. Bush beans, beets, brussels sprouts, kohlrabi, Swiss chard, turnips, leaf lettuce, and collards can be planted until the end of July. Spinach can be planted any time in August. If lima beans and carrots are planted by July 15 and the weather stays warm in the fall, they will produce a crop. Cabbage and broccoli transplants may be set out in the garden in late July, but it is too late to start them from seed. To grow plants from seed, start the seeds in the last half of June.

In preparing beds make sure the soil is not heavily crusted because this makes it difficult for the seedlings to come up. A light mulch can reduce crusting problems, as can proper watering. Do not let the soil surface dry out until the seedlings are up and have formed true leaves.

HARVEST

Vegetables should be harvested when they are young and tender. Zucchini can be picked any time after it is formed but will have the best flavor when it is about six to twelve inches long. If it gets large, the seeds inside will begin to turn hard and inedible. Those zucchini can still be used for stuffing or shredded for zucchini bread after the seeds are removed, but picking the entire crop when it is still small is best.

Beans should be picked when the pods are about pencil width or a little larger but before the beans inside the pods start to enlarge and make the pods look lumpy. If they are not harvested before the pods are lumpy, shell the beans and cook the shelled beans along with the more tender pods. Pick beans every day to get the most tender pods and to keep the plants in production as long as possible.

Beets and carrots can get tough and fibrous if they are left in the ground too long. Examine the crown of the root by pushing a little soil aside. If the beets are about an inch and a half in diameter and the carrots are more than three-quarters of an inch, pull a few. If they are large enough to make a good harvest and still not fibrous, pull the rest of the crop.

Check all crops daily to see what needs to be harvested. Examine them for insects and diseases at the same time. If problems are found and controlled when they first appear, more vegetables of better quality will be produced.

FROST

As long as the temperature doesn't fall more than a few degrees below freezing, the plants in the vegetable garden can be protected. Some plants, like broccoli, cabbage, and carrots can withstand cold temperatures. Their flavor may even be improved by light frost. Tomatoes, cucumbers, squash, and other warm-weather producers will be damaged by the first frost. To protect them have plenty of old sheets, rags, landscape cloth, or newspaper available. When frost is predicted, cover the plants and anchor the covers with rocks so they won't blow away in high winds. This will retain the warmth that is still in the soil inside the covering so the cold air cannot damage the plants. Plastic is not nearly as good an insulator as cloth. Remove the covering the morning after the frost so the sun can warm the plants and soil. If the covers are damp, dry them out during the day.

Once a hard freeze is expected-temperatures below 27°F-pick all the tomatoes, squash, and cucumbers that can be harvested. Cucumbers and squash can be picked if they are large enough to use. Tomatoes can be picked if they have reached mature size and have started to turn lighter green, whitish, or pink.

Once melons and many other fruits are off the plant they do not ripen further. Tomatoes are the only garden produce likely to ripen properly off the vine after a killing frost. Discard the other unripe fruit in the compost pile. Wrap tomatoes that are light green or pink in newspaper and put them in a cool place to slow their ripening process. The tomatoes will not ripen all at once, and the last ones may just be getting ripe at Christmas. Do not put them in the refrigerator or in a place that will get below 50°F or they will rot without ripening.

ORGANIC PRODUCTION

Gardening organically is more than just controlling insects and diseases without chemicals. Organic gardening is an approach that involves the soil, the plants, the immediate surroundings of the plant, and the philosophy of the gardener. Fortunately, it is easier for a gardener to convert to organic methods than for a farmer.

One of the most important steps in organic gardening is plant selection. Choose disease- and insect-resistant plants. Look for information about disease resistance in the description in catalogs and on seed packets. For example, tomatoes should have the initials V and F after the variety name, which means they are resistant to two common wilt diseases. If the soil is sandy, the initial N, for nematode, should also be there.

Diversity and rotation are other ways to resist insect attack or disease. Plant as many species and varieties as you have room for. Choosing different varieties of the same vegetable can prolong the harvest of many plants, like beans or lettuce, as well as increase the likelihood that at least one variety will be resistant to garden pests. Avoid planting all the related vegetables together. For example, separate one variety of beans from another variety with other plants. Mixing herbs and flowers among the vegetables is also helpful. Do not plant your vegetables where a variety of the same family grew last year. Tomatoes, eggplant, chile, and potatoes are in the same family and should be planted in different areas each year. Broccoli, cabbage, cauliflower, and brussels sprouts are also in the same family.

Continually building your soil with organic matter is also important. Organic matter will make the soil rich, water retentive, and easier to work. It will also be easier for the plant roots to penetrate. A good soil that has plenty of nutrients without being overfertilized will help keep the plants healthy, and healthy plants are less likely to be attacked by insects or diseases.

If insects invade the garden, fight them first with mechanical means, such as spraying aphids with cold water or handpicking caterpillars. If that is not effective, purchase biological controls. These are beneficial insects or biological pathogens like BT that can kill the insects. If all

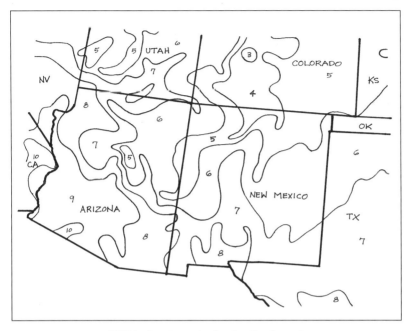

USDA climate zones for the Southwest

these defenses fail, you can try rotenone, pyrethrum, or other organic insecticides. Even though these compounds are derived from plants, they are poisonous in large quantities and should be used according to label directions as with any manufactured pesticide.

ASPARAGUS

Watering once a month through the winter should be sufficient for asparagus unless it is being grown in a very sandy soil. Asparagus likes well-drained soil and can tolerate some dryness except in early spring when the spears are growing. Unusually warm spring weather should make asparagus come up earlier and grow faster although the quality will not be as good. With higher than average rainfall, watering more than once a month in winter could induce root rot or crown rot. Both are common asparagus diseases in heavy soils. Clay soil or soil that is heavily amended with manure or compost can be a problem. In heavy soil, water sparingly except in spring.

BEANS

Separate members of the onion family (garlic, chives, leeks, etc.) from members of the legume family (beans, peas, sweet peas, etc.) The roots of the onion produce an antibiotic substance that is secreted into the soil immediately around the roots. Legumes coexist with a bacteria that forms nodules on their roots and helps them get nitrogen. The antibiotic from the onions kills the legume bacteria.

BROCCOLI

Broccoli needs a long cool period in order to develop properly and produce large, good-tasting heads. Because the temperatures in the Southwest usually rise rapidly in the spring, we have problems growing spring-planted broccoli. Broccoli is better grown in the fall. Start the plants in late June or early July either indoors or in a protected, shady location outside. Set them out in the garden in late July or early August. Make sure they get enough water during the first few weeks. Protect them from early hard freezes in the fall by covering them with sheets or burlap overnight. By mid- to late October, the broccoli will be ready to harvest.

CELERY

Celery requires moist, acid soil with a great deal of organic matter in it. It also requires a long, cool growing season. Those conditions simply do not exist here, and celery is generally not successful in the average southwestern garden.

CHILE

Most chile varieties prefer warmer germination temperatures and germinate a little more slowly than tomatoes. If the temperature of the potting soil is below 65°F, the chiles will be very slow in germinating while the tomatoes will be only slightly slower than at warmer temperatures. At 60°F the chiles could take up to two weeks longer than the tomatoes. On the windowsill the average temperature will be slightly cooler than in the rest of the house, which might be too cold for the chile seed to germinate. Put the pot or flat in a warmer place until the plants start to grow or put a heating cable under the pot. Once the plants have come up, place the pot back on the windowsill where the plants can get plenty of light. Once the seeds have germinated, the plants will be healthier if the temperature is about 70° during the day and 65° at night.

Green chiles and red chiles come from the same plant. Green chiles are not ripe; red chiles are. To determine when to harvest green chiles, watch the fruit as it develops. The flesh starts to get thicker and the gloss on the surface dulls a little just before the fruit is ripe. Red chiles can be harvested any time the color is present.

To make a chile ristra, you will need a bushel of red chiles, some light-weight cotton string, and a wire coat hanger or other heavy wire. Begin by tying clusters of chiles onto the string. To do this, hold three chiles by their stems, wrap the string around the stems twice, bring the string upward between two of the chiles, and pull it tight. Make a half hitch with the string, place it over the three stems, and pull that tight. In the same manner tie three more chile pods about three inches from the first. Continue tying on chiles until you have several clusters or until the weight makes it difficult to handle. Cut the string and start over again. Continue tying until all the chiles are used.

Straighten the coat hanger and suspend the wire from a nail or door-knob. Make a loop in the end of the wire to keep the chiles from slipping off. Starting with the first set of three chiles, braid the chiles around the wire. The process is very similar to braiding hair. Use the wire as one strand and any two chiles as the other strands. As the chiles are braided, push the cluster down in the center so each cluster fits tight against its

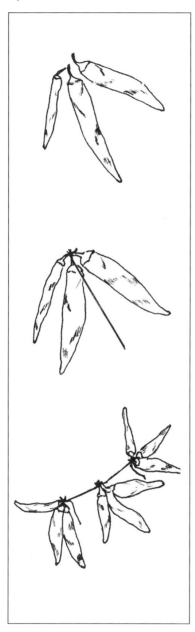

neighbor. Position the chiles to protrude in all directions as you work. Continue braiding until all the chiles have been used.

Unless a chile ristra has been shellacked or painted, the chiles can be used in recipes. The ristra was originally the means of storing dried chiles through the winter. Its decorative qualities were secondary. Hang the ristra outside to dry. If it gets moldy, do not eat the chiles. To use the dried chiles, pull a chile off the ristra, leaving the stem behind. For milder flavor, remove the seeds and veins. Wash off any dust that has accumulated on the chile. Put the pods in a saucepan, cover with water, and boil for about ten minutes, until the pulp separates from the skin. You may let the pods stand in water for an hour then put them through a colander or ricer, or put them in a blender or food processor with the cooking water and blend until a paste is formed. You may substitute tomato juice for some of the water. If you wish, strain the paste before using. You may want to add garlic and onion sautéed in a little olive oil, with vinegar for a tart sauce, or two tablespoons vinegar, four tablespoons brown sugar, and one teaspoon cinnamon for a sweet sauce.

The dried pods can be processed in a blender or food processor to make chile powder.

HORSERADISH

Horseradish is a deep-rooted, persistent plant that can thrive with little care but can be frustrating when it is growing where it isn't wanted. If it is growing in an area with desirable plants the problem is even more difficult. One way to eradicate horseradish is to keep digging the roots and cutting the leaves off just below ground level whenever they appear. This will eventually starve the roots out. Another way to starve the roots is to cover the area with black plastic. Glyphosate (sold under the trade names Kleenup and Roundup) should kill horseradish if it is applied when the horseradish is starting to flower in the summer and once more as the food is being

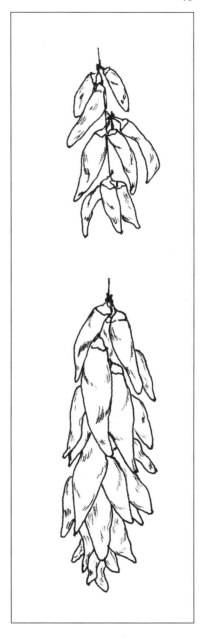

translocated into the roots in the fall. Follow the directions for killing bindweed.

MELONS

Melon seeds from melons eaten last year will grow, but they may not produce the same kind of melon. Melons, cucumbers, squash, and gourds are all in the same family and can cross with each other. They are pollinated by bees, so the seeds of the melon could be a hybrid of that type and any other member of the family growing within the distance one bee could fly. These natural crosses sometimes produce interesting results, and growing and tasting the fruit is worth it if there is adequate space to grow what may turn out to be a large, useless vine. Sometimes the fruit may look like a giant warty gourd on the outside and have delicious melonlike flesh on the inside. Or it may look like a big, sweet cantaloupe on the outside and be tough and fibrous, like a gourd, on the inside. If the melon was produced in the center of a large field of the same type of melons, chances are the fruit will be the same as the melon. If a summerlong gardening adventure sounds like fun, plant the melons and see what is produced.

ONIONS

Onions can be produced three ways: from seeds, sets, or transplants. The easiest way is from sets, although sets are more expensive than seeds. Sets are little onion bulbs that were started the summer before and stored over the winter. Only varieties that can withstand long storage periods are available as sets. They can be set into the ground so their tops are just below the surface in late March. Be sure to put the pointed end up.

The formation of bulbs by onions is influenced by day length. Some types of onions, such as Bermuda onions, begin to form bulbs when they get fifteen to sixteen hours of sunlight a day. Intermediate-day-length onions begin to form bulbs with thirteen to fourteen hours of sunlight a day. Sweet Spanish onions are intermediate. Short-day onions, like

Granex, begin to form bulbs when the days are twelve to thirteen hours long. The onion first produces leaves, then the bulb. The more leaves the onion has before bulb formation starts, the larger the bulb. The most commonly sold onions in this area are intermediate day length.

Onions need to be properly cured, then stored in a cool, dry place. When the fall crop is ready to harvest, dig the onions and put them on top of the ground to dry, covering each onion with the leaves of the next one. Or spread them in a well-ventilated shed. If the weather is damp, they will dry better if they are placed on benches or screens in a shed rather than on the ground. When they are completely dry, select the ones with the smallest necks for storage. Use the ones with larger necks first. Onions harvested in the summer should be used before the fall-harvested ones. Store onions in an area with low humidity and temperatures just above freezing.

How long onions can be stored depends on the type of onion. Some types will last only a few weeks; others will last until new onions come in next year. Bermuda and red onions have a short storage life, whereas several of the yellow onion varieties can be stored for long periods.

Perennial onions are also easy to grow. These are onions that produce bulblets at the top of their leaves every year as well as dividing at the bulb. These do not store particularly well but produce over a long period of time. If there is an area of the yard or garden that could be devoted to long-term onion production, try perennial onions. They can be harvested as green onions almost as soon as the new leaves come up in the spring, or left in the ground and harvested as they get larger throughout the summer. A few seed catalogs have sets for these onions, but the most common means of getting them is from friends or neighbors who have extra bulblets. Once they are started, there will be plenty of bulblets to share.

POTATOES

Locally grown potatoes often have scaly patches, or scab. The scabs, which can be either raised or pitted, are caused by a fungus that is common in soil where potatoes have been grown for several years. The potatoes are more susceptible to infection if the pH is above 5.3, as almost all southwestern soils are. Crop rotation and resistant varieties are the best solutions to the problem. Varieties that are resistant to scab include Alamo, Cherokee, Superior, Ona, Russet Rural, Russet Burbank, Norland, Sioux, and Chieftain. Even with these varieties it is best to grow potatoes in a given area only once every four years.

PUMPKINS AND WINTER SQUASH

Pumpkins take from 90 to 120 days from planting to ripen. Generally the larger varieties ripen later. Plant the seeds of a shorter-season variety by June 20 to have a few pumpkins before Halloween. The biggest danger to pumpkins is squash bugs. They carry a bacterial wilt disease that kills the vines. Constant vigilance is needed to keep ahead of the squash bugs.

To grow really big pumpkins, buy seeds of the right variety. Atlantic Giant, Big Max, and Howden are all large varieties. To grow big pumpkins, you will need to supply plenty of fertilizer and water. Dig lots of manure or compost into the soil along with about a quarter of a cup of garden fertilizer for each vine, and give the plants plenty of space. The vines can spread as much as twenty-five feet. Once a month scratch about two tablespoons of garden fertilizer with plenty of nitrogen in it into the soil around the vine. Encourage the vines to root in several places so they can get nutrients from a number of sources. If the main vine is attacked by insects or disease, some parts may survive.

When the pumpkin sets fruit, remove all but one of the fruits from each section of the vine. This will allow all the plant's energy to go into producing a few large pumpkins. Pumpkins can take light frosts but will keep longer if they are harvested before frost. Because the big pumpkins take about 120 days to mature, they should be planted early and cannot be grown at the higher altitudes where the growing season is less than 120 days.

Winter squash are ready to harvest when the skin is tough and can't be punctured by a fingernail. Cut the mature squash off the vine with about an inch of the stem still attached. This will reduce the chances of rot and the squash can be stored for a longer period of time. Pumpkins can be picked any time after they are fully orange. Leave a portion of the stem on those, too, for the jack-o'-lantern's handle or for longer storage.

Pumpkins and squash should be stored at about 55°F in a dry place. Warmer temperatures allow them to spoil more quickly and cooler temperatures may cause sunken brown spots on the surface. These spots are caused by the breakdown of the enzymes in the fruit not bacteria or fungal rot organisms, but those rot organisms can easily invade the fruit through the spots.

RADISHES

Several factors affect the size and quality of radishes. Radishes and other root crops need to be grown in a loose soil with plenty of potassium fertilizer. Since many southwestern soils are already high in potassium, have the soil tested before adding potassium fertilizer. Radishes do not need much nitrogen, and excess nitrogen can cause problems, such as large, healthy leaves but not much root. If the soil is deficient in nitrogen, add slightly less than the amount recommended for vegetables. If nitrogen fertilizer or manure have regularly been added, cut down on applications in the radish bed for a couple of years. Plant radishes in spring or fall. They will not do well if planted after the weather gets hot. Thinning radishes is important. Large, well-shaped radishes will not be produced unless the plants are thinned so they are about two inches apart. Radishes need a steady supply of water and nutrients to grow rapidly, so be sure to irrigate frequently. If these suggestions do not produce tasty, round radishes, try a different variety. The long white icicle radishes can sometimes tolerate our climate better than some of the round red varieties.

RHUBARB

In most regions rhubarb corms are divided in early spring, although they can be divided and replanted in late fall. To divide the rhubarb, dig up the entire clump, shake off the soil and cut it into pieces. Each piece should have at least one strong, healthy eye, or bud. Enrich the soil with plenty of organic matter dug in to a depth of at least a foot, then replant the corms. They should be planted about three or four inches deep, so the buds are about two inches below the surface. Space the plants two to three feet apart depending on the fertility of the soil. Do not harvest the stalks the first year. Let the plant use that energy to become well established. After that cut the thickest stalks off each year. Do not take more than half the stalks from the plant in any one year.

Rhubarb prefers frozen soil in winter and cool seasons. In the high desert, plant rhubarb in partial shade to keep it a little cooler and mulch well around the plant. The Canadian red variety of rhubarb is adapted to colder weather than we have here and becomes too stressed by our hot weather to survive.

SPINACH

Spinach planted in early spring often grows very slowly. Cold temperatures could stop the growth of plants, although even temperatures slightly below freezing will not kill spinach. Slow-growing spinach may lack nitrogen. Southwestern soils tend to be low in nitrogen, and cold weather makes the nitrogen less available, particularly if organic or slow-release sources are used. Apply nitrogen fertilizer before planting.

SWEET POTATOES

Sweet potatoes are tuberous roots. Sweet potato plants are started from shoots pulled off a mature, sprouted sweet potato. Generally the more-rounded end is the stem end and should go up, while the more-pointed root end should go down. If you are unsure which end is which, lay the root on its side in a deep pan, like a loaf pan. Add water until it half covers the root and wait for it to sprout.

TOMATOES

Leggy tomato plants, and many other plants with a long central stem, can be placed on their side in a trench for planting. Remove the lowest set of leaves from the stem, dig a short trench rather than a round hole for planting, and lay the plant on its side in the trench. Bend the stem gently so the remaining leaves are above the ground, then cover the stem. The stem will sprout roots and increase the ability of the plants to absorb water and nutrients from the soil. Do not do this with plants like lettuce or cabbage, which grow from a crown rather than a long stem.

The current recommendations for early tomatoes are Early Girl, Early Pick VF, Extra Early VFNT, and Fantastic. Later varieties include Beefmaster VFN, Better Boy VFN, Heinz 1350, and Homestead 24. Beefmaster and Better Boy are large tomatoes. The letters after the names indicate disease and pest resistance. V means the variety is resistant to verticillium wilt; F means resistance to fusarium wilt. Both problems are rather common, and resistant varieties should be selected. N indicates nematode resistance, which is important if nematodes are a problem or the soil is sandy. The T means resistance to tobacco mosaic virus. In this area, the virus is spread most often by smokers who handle plants without washing their hands with soap and water.

The most important factor in producing early tomatoes is to buy a variety that produces fruit in a short period of time. These usually produce small tomatoes, not the large hamburger size. Start them early or buy large plants at the store.

Before planting be sure the plants are hardened off. Place them outside during the day and let the soil dry out somewhat. Bring them inside at night if cold weather is expected and water them before the plants wilt. After about a week they should be ready to plant outside. If the plants are set out into the garden without being hardened off they will go into shock, stop growing, drop all their flowers, and possibly even die.

Once outside, the plants can be covered with a plastic or glass cover like a greenhouse. Be sure to prop the cover up on bright sunny days so there is some air circulation. Otherwise the plants might bake. You can also protect the plants with a wall of water, which is a plastic ring that has long pockets in it. When the pockets are filled with water, the water gives off heat as the temperature falls below freezing. This can keep the tomatoes alive at temperatures well below freezing. Another technique is to dig a large hole and plant the tomato in the bottom of the hole so the top of the plant barely shows above the surface of the soil. Put a piece of glass or plastic over the top, or simply cover the hole on cold nights with wood or paper weighted down on the edges. As the weather becomes more settled and the tomato plant grows taller, gradually fill in the hole with soil. This insures a deeper, more extensive root system and makes the plant able to withstand dry periods in the summer, as well as protecting it from spring frosts.

Pinching off the side branches of the tomato vine will produce larger tomatoes, although there will be fewer of them. With our bright sunlight, fruit on pinched vines will be susceptible to sunscald. Either cage the tomatoes or let them sprawl on the ground to avoid sunscald. If they sprawl on the ground, sow bugs may eat part of the fruit or it may rot when the soil is wet, but there will be plenty of leaves to shade the fruit. Probably the best way to produce tomatoes is to let them grow in cages without pinching them. This gets the fruit off the ground, out of the irrigation water, and out of reach of sow bugs. The leaves will be packed tighter, for better shade, if the tomatoes are caged. Use purchased cages or any wire with holes large enough to reach through and pull the fruit out. To produce larger tomatoes, remove some of the flower clusters rather than entire branches.

The development of tomatoes takes place in several stages, and tem-perature plays an important role in all of them. More flowers are developed when night temperatures are between 55 and 60°F. Therefore more tomatoes are set on the plant early in the season than in midsummer. Just before frost another large flush of flowers will set fruit, but they won't have time to ripen. High temperatures, above 94°F, also reduce the viability of tomato pollen, so very few tomatoes are set in hot weather. The tomatoes that ripen in midsummer were set on the plant before the weather got hot. When all these have ripened, there may be a short break in tomato production before the tomatoes that set on after the weather has cooled will be ready for harvest. The red pigment in tomatoes does not develop when temperatures are above 86°F. As temperatures rise above that point, less and less pigment will develop. The orange tomatoes that are produced at high temperatures are just as good as the red tomatoes and can be used in the same ways.

Whole, unblemished tomatoes can be frozen for later use. Simply wash them, put them in a plastic bag, and freeze them. In the winter, take them out of the freezer and run warm water over them. The peel will slip right off. Either thaw and cut the tomato or add whole tomatoes to soups or stews.

Two viruses cause yellow streaks running down tomatoes, as do spider mites. First check for spider mites by picking a small branch of the tomato plant and shaking it vigorously over a piece of white paper. Little spots moving around on the paper indicate spider mites. They can be controlled with a miticide or by washing the plant with water daily. Spider mites attack a number of plants, so look for evidence of damage on other plants in the garden.

If there are no little moving spots on the paper and the problem is confined to one or two plants, it is probably a virus. The virus can be spread by insects from the plant it is on to healthy plants. There is no practical cure for the virus, and the plants should be removed from the garden. The tomatoes can be eaten with no problem if you do not mind the appearance.

Two fungi, *Rhizoctonia* root rot and *Phytopthera*, cause wilting of chile and tomato plants from the bottom up. Generally, these fungi occur in spots and may not be affecting all the plants in the garden. They are soil fungi that increase under moist conditions. Take care when watering the plants that the root zone is moistened but there is no standing water. The fungi cannot be controlled with fungicides and severely affected plants should be removed.

Viral wilts can cause wilting from the top down. These viral wilts also cause spots or deformity of leaves. Viral wilts cannot be controlled except by controlling the insects that carry them and removing the plants on which they overwinter. Spotted wilt virus entered New Mexico in the early 1990s and spread rapidly throughout the state. It is spread by sucking insects and has been shown to overwinter on bindweed and curly dock. Control of insects and weeds is recommended.

Tomatoes, squash, cucumbers, melons, and other vegetables often start to rot at the end where the blossom was. This is called blossom end rot. Mulch is the best defense against blossom end rot. Blossom end rot is the result of an irregular supply of water. Even if the plants are watered frequently, the soil can dry out enough on a hot summer day to trigger blossom end rot. A thick organic mulch will keep the soil evenly moist and reduce the amount of irrigation water needed.

Aphids are the most common insects on tomatoes. Examine the plants regularly for aphids or other insects and wash them off with a hose when they appear. If they get out of hand, other control measures should be used. Aphids on tomatoes can be controlled with insecticidal soaps, malathion, pyrethrins, Diazinon, or dimethoate (Cygon). These chemicals vary in toxicity and effectiveness. Follow directions carefully when any pesticide is used.

Tomato worms can also be a problem. They are large green worms, the larvae of sphinx moths that can quickly strip tomato stems of leaves. They should either be picked off the plant and smashed or treated with an insecticide. They are often difficult to find because the worm itself looks like a tomato stem.

Tomatoes continue to produce fruit until the plant is frozen. See the map on page 163 for the average first-frost date. Tomatoes and many other plants can be protected from mild frosts by covering them with an old sheet, piece of plastic, or other protective covering. Be sure to remove the covering when the sun comes out in the morning. When heavy frost is predicted, harvest all the tomatoes on the vine that show any pink coloration. Those that have lost their green color and are rather whitish but not pink yet will ripen if harvested and kept in a paper bag at room temperature. Do not put them in a window sill or they may get over-heated and sunscald.

When a heavy frost does come and the tomato vines are wilted and begin to turn black, the green tomatoes can be harvested from the vine for making relish or other green tomato dishes. After all the green fruit is harvested, pull the vines and dispose of them in the compost pile or trash. Do not leave them in the garden as diseases may overwinter on the vines.

ZUCCHINI

Many varieties of squash, along with cucumbers, produce male flowers first then start producing female flowers. In order to get fruit, there must be both male and female flowers and bees to carry the pollen from the male to the female flower. The production of female flowers depends on the maturity of the vine, day length, and temperature. Even before female flowers are pollinated, they have a tiny fruit between the stem and the flower. Not all female flowers will set fruit. The vine produces more than it can support, so some drop off even if there is good pollination. However a good crop of squash should be produced soon after female flowers start to appear.

Zucchini has many uses. Fresh zucchini can be served in salads, cut up and eaten raw like cucumber slices or carrot sticks, used in soups or stews, baked, pickled, sautéed, or grated for use in zucchini bread, cake, or cookies. Recipes are available in most cookbooks.

GOURDS

Gourds are less likely to rot if they are harvested before frost. They can be harvested any time after they reach mature size, have the decorative coloring characteristic of the variety, and have a hard shell. Leave a small section of the stem on the gourds when they are cut, wash them in a diluted solution of household bleach, and dry them with a towel. Place them in a single layer in a well-ventilated place for four to six weeks to make sure they are completely dry, then spray with a clear varnish or lacquer to preserve them.

HERBS

Parsley, basil, and cilantro are easy herbs to grow from seed. All will do best in full sun and well-drained soil. Prepare the soil thoroughly by digging in generous supplies of organic matter to a depth of at least twelve inches. Seeds are available at any garden outlet. Follow the directions on the package for planting times. The beds should be mulched to prevent the soil from drying out. Parsley can be a perennial if it is not overharvested and seed heads are removed. If allowed to go to seed in late summer, basil will reseed itself.

Chives, savory, sage, peppermint, rosemary, sweet marjoram, and thyme are among the perennial herbs most likely to do well in our soils. All require moderate amounts of water. Again, prepare the soil thoroughly. Buy plants when they are available in the nurseries. Be sure to allow enough space when they are planted and provide plenty of water at first. All these herbs are quite hardy and will not need extra protection once they are established.

Comfrey has been used as a remedy for a number of ailments. Although some claims of its healing power are extravagant, it is high in calcium, phosphorus, potassium, and trace minerals, as well as vitamins A and C. It is a source of allantoin, which is useful in treating burns, wounds, and ulcers. Young comfrey leaves can be eaten like spinach or used in salads. The leaves also make good livestock feed.

The comfrey plant grows two or three feet high and has rough, hairy stems and leaves. The lower leaves are about the size and shape of a donkey's ears. They become somewhat smaller higher on the stem. The flowers are creamy yellow or purple blue. The first flowers appear in late spring, and the plant continues blooming through most of the summer. Comfrey leaves will stay green after many other plants have been killed by frost.

Comfrey is propagated by dividing established plants or from root cuttings. Divisions should be planted so the crown is at the soil surface. Roots should be planted three to six inches deep in soil that has been well tilled. The roots should be placed horizontally in a trench. Space plants or cuttings three feet apart each way.

Comfrey is a perennial that spreads easily. New plants will grow from only a small section of root, making it a difficult plant to eradicate once it is established. It may be best to sink an old metal tub or bucket into the ground and grow the comfrey in that in order to contain it.

Japanese research has shown that alkaloids purified from natural comfrey may cause liver cancer in rats if they are used in large enough quantities. Another interpretation of the same research seems to indicate that the comfrey has a protective quality and the rats were prone to liver cancer even without the comfrey alkaloid. Some countries have reacted by banning comfrey from herbal preparations. Anyone who suspects they may be prone to liver cancer because of family history or other indications should probably avoid eating comfrey.

Almost any herb can be grown in a sunny area indoors, but several will become too large for the windowsill before the end of the winter.

Chive is a favorite windowsill herb. Leaves can be snipped off as they are needed. Remember to leave about two inches of leaves on the plant so it can resume growing. Basil is another popular plant for windowsill culture. If the leaves are pinched off often enough, the plant will remain small and bushy. Use basil leaves in any dish containing tomatoes.

Catnip can also be grown on the windowsill. Generally, a cat will notice the catnip only if the leaves are cut or bruised. If the plant is pruned, be sure to give the cuttings to the cat, or she will be on the windowsill looking for the plant and may knock all the pots on the floor.

Other herbs that do well indoors are parsley, savory, and thyme. They can be grown from seeds, but quicker results can be achieved by buying or digging plants. If a plant is dug from the yard, prune it back extensively before bringing it inside. Take care not to overwater herbs. Many prefer the soil slightly on the dry side. They will keep producing new, aromatic leaves as long as they are pinched or pruned, so use them generously once the plants are established on the windowsill.

It is possible to grow some herbs, particularly rosemary, as a standard form. A standard form is a shrub, vine, or herbaceous plant trained to grow in treelike form. To train rosemary to grow as a standard, first be sure it is a full-size, upright rosemary shrub, not a dwarf or prostrate variety. Select a long, sturdy branch of that shrub and prune the others back. Stake the selected branch in an upright position. Use a stake that is as tall as the stem of the standard will be. Tie the branch with enough plant ties that it will stand upright but no more than are necessary to get a relatively straight trunk. Keep the ties slightly loose so the plant can grow but tight enough to keep the stem upright.

When the branch reaches the top of the stake, cut off the lower side branches and pinch back the top growth to make it grow bushy and balllike. When a ball of foliage has grown at the top of the branch, cut off all the lower growth so the trunk below the ball of top growth is bare. As time goes on, this trunk will become thicker and stronger. As it does, remove the ties, and when it will stand on its own, remove the stake. Continue pinching the top growth to keep it bushy. As the trunk grows in diameter, allow the top to grow into a slightly larger ball. Several years are required to form a self-supporting standard from any plant, but rosemary is relatively fast growing and should stand on its own more quickly than many other plants.

Pesticides and Plant Problems

One of the most perplexing issues in contemporary agriculture is pesticide use and pesticide residues on produce. Our food is safer now than it was when ergot fungus was uncontrollable on grain and led to the poisoning of thousands of Europeans. Our water is safer now that we can control rodents and fleas so that the plague is a rarity. We also have more food available in the world—enough to feed everyone on the planet if it were distributed properly. This is partly because of the development of insecticides that reduced the amount of human food being eaten by insects. A by-product of this is that we have gotten used to inexpensive, blemish-free food; we expect to buy apples without worms and potatoes without maggots.

The pesticides that give us all this, however, are poisonous. Some are only mildly poisonous. Malathion, for example, is half as poisonous as aspirin. Others are extremely toxic. Some remain in the ground for years at a time. We are still having problems with DDT and can expect it to remain in our food chain for many more years. Others, like glyphosate, are inactivated as soon as they come in contact with the ground.

Some agriculture chemicals have been shown to cause cancer in rats. Breakdown products and inert ingredients of pesticide formulations are also tested for their ability to cause cancer. For example, Alar, which caused a scare because of its use on apples and was banned, is a synthetic formulation of a growth regulator that occurs naturally in apples. It does not cause cancer. It does, however, break down into a chemical called UDMH, which can, in large doses, cause cancer. The doses of UDMH known to cause cancer are toxic in other ways. Children would fail to gain weight and would have liver problems before they got cancer from such high doses. The research is not in yet on the effects of lower doses of UDMH.

Spot checks are done on fruits and vegetables sold by commercial outlets. These checks have shown that 80 to 85 percent of the produce sold in national markets have no pesticide residues; 10 to 15 percent have less than one-tenth the minimum tolerance, which is 1 percent. The rest are generally between one-tenth tolerance and the minimum tolerance levels. Every once in a while, produce is found on which pesticide levels exceed minimum tolerance levels. When this happens it makes the news and becomes the basis for a new pesticide scare. On the average, however, produce contains pesticide residues at or below the minimum safety tolerance set by the EPA.

The greater danger comes from misuse of chemicals in home gardens and yards. In this regard, each individual must decide how much risk he or she is willing to take. Just because malathion is less toxic than aspirin doesn't mean it should be handled carelessly. Too many aspirin can kill, just as too much malathion can. Always read and follow the directions on the label. Sometimes those directions can be confusing. If they are, ask someone else to help you decipher them. Do not use "a little extra" of any pesticide. It could kill things that should not be killed.

Before buying a product, read the label and make sure it will do what needs to be done. Look for the words *pesticide, caustic, acid, corrosive, oxidizer, poison, flammable, warning,* or *danger* on the label. Any of these words signal that the chemical can be potentially hazardous. Exposure to hazardous materials can produce reactions that may include dizziness, nausea, shortness of breath, headaches, sweating, blurred vision, burns, and skin or eye irritation. Some products contain known or suspected carcinogens.

If a chemical with one of the words listed above on it is purchased, be responsible for using and disposing of it properly. Do not buy more than is needed for immediate use. If the chemical requires mixing and is needed in a different quantity than that given on the label, such as mixing a quart when the directions are for a gallon, double-check calculations before mixing. If necessary, find someone to help or call your county extension agent.

One of the most common causes of home accidents is the release of toxic gasses from combining chemicals that should not be mixed. Chemicals should be combined only when specific directions for mixing them are on the label.

Always use the safest material or procedure available. The use of fungicides can be reduced by proper watering and keeping garden areas clean. Soap and water or old dishwater is an effective treatment for many minor insect infestations. A little hoeing or digging early in the season can mean much less herbicide use later in the season.

Dispose of wastes carefully and correctly. The Albuquerque Environmental Health Department collects household hazardous waste. In the spring, be sure to include the garage, garden shed, and other storage areas in the spring cleaning effort. Take any hazardous chemicals to the collection point.

Most products have at least a two-year shelf life once they have been opened. Proper storage methods are important. Powdered pesticides such as rose dust may absorb moisture and become unusable. Discard dry pesticides that have not been properly stored or are over two years old.

Liquids will not absorb moisture, but careful storage is still important. Greatly fluctuating temperatures may affect the ability of the active ingredient to remain dissolved in the water. Products should not be stored in front of a window or in direct sunlight.

If the directions for use are no longer available, discard the chemical. Do not pour it down the sink or into the gutter. Contact your county agent for directions if the identity of the chemical is known. If not, contact the Environmental Health Department of the city or county. Treat any unidentified garden chemicals as hazardous materials.

If any pesticides, fertilizers, or other chemicals are leaking out of the container, carefully place the entire leaking container into another container. Dispose of the entire container in the appropriate manner. Fertilizers that will not be used can be disposed of in a sanitary landfill. Fungicides, herbicides, insecticides, rat poison, weed killers, and anything with the words *poison* or *danger* on the label should be taken to the hazardous waste collection point.

Just because something is labeled organic does not mean it is not toxic. Nicotine sulfate is an organic pesticide that is more toxic to humans than several manufactured pesticides. Know what precautions to take before using any pesticide, organic or manufactured. These can be found on the label or in the little booklet that comes with the pesticide. If used properly, pesticides are less dangerous than the drive to the store to buy the pesticides. But carelessness with pesticides invites trouble.

If used properly, most organic pesticides are effective. Their safety varies. Commonly used plant-derived pesticides include sabadilla, pyrethrin, rotenone, and nicotine. Sabadilla is derived from the seed of a lily-like plant from the Caribbean. Its toxicity comes from a group of alkaloids known as veratrine. Sabadilla is one of the most effective defenses against squash bugs. It can irritate mucous membranes, so avoid breathing the dust.

Pyrethrins are derived from the flowers of a plant of the chrysanthemum family. The plant is sometimes called painted daisy. It is a contact insecticide that is effective against soft-bodied insects. Natural pyrethrin is one of the least toxic insecticides to humans and other warm-blooded animals. Be sure to keep it out of bodies of water to avoid killing fish, and do not dispose of containers where residue can be washed into the water. Pyrethrin kills by rapidly paralyzing insects. It is usually mixed with a synergist like piperonyl butoxide that makes the pyrethrin more toxic to insects so the insecticide is effective at economical rates.

Rotenone can be isolated from a variety of plants. It is harmless to plants, moderately toxic to most warm-blooded animals, but extremely toxic to swine and fish. In fact, it is used to kill fish, both by South American Indians to make fishing easier and by North American wildlife specialists and fish farmers to eliminate undesired fish in controlled stocking situations. Rotenone is a broad-spectrum insecticide that can be used against many garden insects, lice, ticks, and spiders. Synergists are also used with rotenone in some formulations. Pyrethrin and rotenone used together are toxic to bees.

Nicotine is sometimes used as a contact poison for sucking insects. It is extremely toxic to humans and is no longer produced in the United States. Some people attempt to make their own extract from tobacco, and a small quantity is imported from India. Avoid using nicotine, as almost any insecticide off the shelf is safer.

Some mineral and manufactured pesticides are considered organic. Diatomaceous earth is a mineral insecticide, and insecticidal soaps and horticultural oils are manufactured pesticides that are generally accepted for organic gardening. Diatomaceous earth is actually the remains of primitive algae with concentrated silica in their bodies. The sedimentary deposits of diatomaceous earth are almost pure silica. When it is ground, the small silica particles are razor sharp and cause tiny abrasions on soft-bodied insects, which subsequently become dehydrated. It can have the same effect on the lungs if large quantities of the dust are inhaled. Be sure to wear a dust mask when using it. Insecticidal soaps are long carbon chain soaps. At mild concentrations, they are toxic to insects; at heavier concentrations, they are toxic to plants. Used at proper concentrations on nonsensitive plants, they are effective against aphids, mealy bugs, and a few other insects but are harmless to humans. Horticulture oils are effective against scale and other insects that don't move much. The insects are covered by a coat of oil and suffocate.

Biological controls may also be considered organic pesticides. These are either living organisms or derivatives from living organisms that are predators of or parasites to the undesirable insects. They are frequently specific to the insect or insect family they control. Many of them are on the market, although only a few are available at traditional garden sup-ply centers. They generally have to be ordered from catalogs. An excep-tion is BT or *Bacillus thuringiensis*, which is available at most garden supply centers. These microorganisms make insects ill but have no effect on humans. There are BT formulations that are specific to moth and but-terfly larvae, mosquito larvae, and elm leaf beetle. They must be used when the larvae are present to be effective.

The most active area of pest control research at this time is genetic engineering. Plants are being developed that have natural resistance or natural pest toxicity built in to them. In the future, we may see less need for any type of pesticide, organic or otherwise.

Chemicals an unlicensed individual can use in a greenhouse are quite limited. Proper watering and sanitation will reduce the need to use pes-ticides. Diseased plant portions can be removed and insects wiped off leaves when pest populations are small. Insecticidal soaps and houseplant insect killers containing resmethrin are effective if used early enough. Before buying any chemical read the entire label carefully to determine whether the chemical will do what needs to be done, if it can be used indoors, and if the material is too toxic to be used safely. The label will also tell how, when, and in what quantities to apply the chemical. Store all chemicals in a locked cabinet and dispose of empty containers accord-ing to the directions on the label.

If pets or children will be in the greenhouse frequently, investigate biological controls and avoid the use of most toxic chemicals. Predators

such as lady bugs, predator mites, or wasps can hold many pest populations to a reasonable level and are available through greenhouse and garden supply catalogs. If fish are in the greenhouse, avoid the use of rotenone,
which is quite toxic to fish.

If properly diluted, Safers Soap is a safe insecticide. In higher concentrations, it causes burning on the leaves of many plants. Flower varieties that are highly or moderately sensitive include zinnias, gaillardia,
cosmos, cornflower, coleus, columbine, chrysanthemum, aster, ageratum,
impatiens, celosia, nasturtium, Shasta daisy, nicotiana, phlox, and viola.
Herbs that are affected include lemon balm, marjoram, oregano, and parsley. Portulaca, lemon and opal basil, ornamental kale, tarragon, salvia,
petunia, dusty miller, pansy, money plant, and calendula are less susceptible but are still affected.

Dormant oil spray can be applied any time the temperatures are not
expected to go above 80°F or fall below 30°F. It should be used on all
fruit trees and on other trees and shrubs known to be susceptible to attack
by scale, mealybugs, or red spider mites. It can be mixed with certain
other insecticides to increase control.

Sevin is a brand name for the insecticide carbaryl. It is used to control a variety of garden pests including cabbage caterpillars, Colorado
potato beetles, Mexican bean beetles, corn earworms, squash bugs, and
tomato hornworm. It can be used on many vegetables up to the day of
harvest. Read the label carefully and follow the instructions exactly. Be
sure to wash the produce before eating it. Do not use Sevin inside the
house. Because it is toxic to bees, use it around dusk when bees have
returned to the hive. Be sure to use all garden dusts and sprays when the
wind is calm.

Glyphosate is less dangerous to people, animals, soil, and water than
most other herbicides. Glyphosate, sold under the trade names Roundup
or Kleenup, is a chemical that attacks certain proteins in plants and is
relatively nontoxic to other living things. The surfactant mixed with the

herbicide is more toxic than the herbicide, but the toxicity research is based on the formulation of the herbicide and surfactant together. It can cause skin irritation to people and animals. If it is spilled on the skin, it should be washed off immediately. The acute toxicity if it is consumed is about the same as vodka. A grown man would have to drink a quart of the concentrate or several gallons of the diluted solution for it to be toxic. As with all chemicals, store glyphosate out of reach of children. Half a cup of the concentrated form could kill a thirty-pound child. If a child drinks concentrated glyphosate, provide water or milk immediately and get medical attention.

Glyphosate is very soluble in water, but is not a danger to our groundwater because it is inactivated when it hits the soil. It immediately binds to soil particles and is quickly broken down by soil microorganisms that see it as a good food source rather than a poison. Populations of certain soil microorganisms increase after use of glyphosate. This does not mean it should be used carelessly. It can cause serious problems if allowed to contaminate bodies of water, by killing water plants and making the water toxic for fish and wildlife. Do not apply it directly to streams or ponds.

Glyphosate is a broad-spectrum herbicide. It can kill most plants if it is applied to the leaves. It cannot be used to control weeds in lawns as it will kill the weeds and the lawn. It will kill difficult perennial weeds if applied properly. It only kills plants that have green leaves. New seeds will sprout, and because there is no residual effect from glyphosate, they will not be affected.

POLLUTION

A great deal of discussion lately has centered on the effect of plants on pollution and the greenhouse effect. While much is known about various types of pollution and the local effect of plants on different pollutants, less is known about the greenhouse effect.

The most severe air pollution problems we have in the Southwest are particulate matter, or dust and pollen, and carbon monoxide. A few places in New Mexico have sulfur dioxide pollution problems, particularly San Juan and Lea Counties. Roswell has an average of about one hundred times as much sulfur dioxide in the air as Albuquerque, but even Roswell does not violate EPA standards for sulfur.

Plants can help prevent and reduce dust pollution. Dust is a localized problem around dirt roads, bare earth school yards, vacant lots, and recently tilled fields. A ground cover of any type, including weeds, helps reduce wind erosion and dust pollution. Plants also serve as dust traps. Although broadleaf plants stop more of the larger dust particles, the particles can become airborne again when the wind blows. Evergreen trees hold onto the particles they stop and thus have a greater effect on dust reduction.

Plants cause suspended particle pollution in the form of pollen. Fungus spores are also found in the air in large quantities in certain seasons. Some weeds and trees are prolific producers of pollen, such as Siberian elm, female junipers, and the weed kochia. Plants with hairy or sticky leaves remove small particles and pollen from the air most effectively. Because many native plants have hairy leaves to reduce water loss, they also collect large amounts of pollen. A single row of trees will filter up to 30 percent of the pollen from the air, while three hundred feet into a forest, 80 percent of the pollen has been filtered out.

Carbon monoxide is also a major New Mexico pollutant in the Southwest. It is released by the incomplete combustion of fuels in furnaces and cars. The most severe problems occur in the winter when more carbon monoxide is produced and temperature inversions trap it in the valleys. Carbon monoxide is not very water soluble, so it is not washed from the air by rainwater and not readily absorbed by plants. Soil fungi and bacteria do, however, remove carbon monoxide from the air. These fungi and bacteria are more plentiful in acid, organic soils, and are more active above 50°F. The effect of soil bacteria on carbon monoxide in cold desert soils is minimal.

Plants do absorb sulfur dioxide and nitrous oxides from the air, and these pollutants dissolve in rainwater, causing acid rain. These are industrial pollutants that are not found in large quantities in most of the Southwest. The exception is those areas that produce oil and electricity. In the energy-producing counties, sulfur dioxide may be found in large enough quantities at certain times to have toxic effects on plants. Where these pollutants are present in less than toxic doses, they seem to change the amino acid availability in the plants and might possibly be responsible for larger numbers of healthier insects.

The greenhouse effect has been debated for several years. Most experts are now in agreement that it exists, but no consensus has been reached on its effects. Numerous models have been created indicating that some areas will be wetter and some drier, that most areas will be warmer, and that the composition of the atmosphere will continue to change. Carbon dioxide is increasing in the atmosphere. Plants need carbon dioxide to survive, and if they have adequate water and mineral nutrition they will grow faster in the presence of extra carbon dioxide. This could counteract the greenhouse effect. However, some scientists say a massive die-off of trees will occur because of temperature changes, which will actually decrease the number of plants absorbing carbon dioxide and add to the problem. We can prepare for this possibility by planting things in new areas. Try planting things that grow in even warmer, drier areas. Plant as many different plants as possible in yards, along streets, and in parks. Then take care of the plants so that as many survive as possible, whatever the climate does. Even if we don't have dramatic climatic changes, having more well-cared for plants in our environment can't hurt.

PESTS

Many people trap snails in dishes of stale beer. The snails seem to be attracted to the beer, crawl in, then can't crawl out. A rotting board can also be put down in the garden. Snails will crawl under it, and it can then be picked up and disposed of. To avoid dealing with the snails on that direct a level, you can use commercial snail baits. Be sure to use them where pets and children will not get into them. To reduce the snail population, keep the area as dry as possible. Eliminating snails in a thick bed of ivy is probably impossible, but the population can be reduced by keeping the area dry.

Whiteflies are one of the most difficult pests we have. There are several species, subspecies, and varieties of whiteflies, and they are all very persistent insects. Whiteflies are small sucking insects that generally feed on the underside of the leaves. If there is a heavy infestation, they can look like a white cloud around the plants when they are disturbed.

Several problems are associated with whiteflies. The first is physical damage to plants caused by the insects' inserting their sucking mouthparts into the leaf. Another is the production of large amounts of honeydew. The larvae feed on plant sap that has lots of sugar and not much protein. In order to concentrate the protein, the larvae excrete the sugar as honeydew, which then encourages the growth of unsightly fungus. Adults and larvae can pick up viruses from infected plants; when adults move on to uninfected plants the virus can be spread.

The adult females lay eggs on the underside of the leaves. Five to twelve days later, depending on how warm it is, the eggs hatch into the crawler stage. Crawlers move around until they find a good feeding place, then insert their mouthparts into the leaf to feed. The crawler remains in the same place until adulthood. As the crawler grows it molts, leaving tiny transparent insect skeletons on infested leaves. After three molts it pupates and later emerges as an adult to mate and reproduce. A female can lay up to three hundred eggs in her lifetime. The entire life cycle is completed in sixteen to thirty-five days. Thus the population can grow very rapidly. One whitefly could have 1 billion descendants in half a year.

Two other factors make it difficult to eliminate whiteflies. First, all

stages of the life cycle can be occurring at the same time. But insecticides are effective only against certain stages, so it takes several sprays
to get rid of the whiteflies. Second, females do not have to mate to lay
viable eggs. Unmated females lay eggs that produce only male offspring.

Of the many species of whiteflies and races within species, some are
simple to eliminate and some almost impossible. When insecticides are
used to eliminate the easy-to-kill types, the difficult-to-kill variety may
increase the next year. Whiteflies are much less common in areas with
long, severe winters and more common in areas where the weather never
dips below freezing.

Whiteflies are attracted to the color yellow. Mix vegetable oil and glycerine, half and half, and spread it on a board painted bright yellow. The
whiteflies get trapped in the oil and glycerine. When the boards are covered with insects, wash them off and recoat them. Yellow sticky boards
are also available at garden shops and nursery supply centers.

Insecticidal soaps are also effective for short periods of time in controlling whiteflies. Effective soaps are those with sixteen or eighteen carbon chains, identified on the label as C16 or C18. A dilute solution of
the soap will kill insects; a strong solution will kill plants. If experimenting
with soaps that are not premixed and labeled as insecticides, start with
a very dilute solution.

Several other manufactured pesticides are labeled for whiteflies. Be
sure the affected plants are on the label before spraying them. Following
label instructions is particularly important when trying to eliminate pests
on food plants. Conventional pesticides are generally effective against
adult whiteflies but do not affect the immature stages; pesticides must be
applied frequently until all stages have reached adulthood. Malathion
and Diazinon can be used against whiteflies. Be sure to wet the underside of the leaf with the insecticide. The whitefly's habit of hiding under
the leaves makes effective control with insecticides even more difficult.

Pesticide-resistant whiteflies are developing due to overuse of pesticides. Farmers are using floating row covers of lightweight woven mate-

rial to protect crops from damage or releasing parasites. The parasites help keep whitefly populations within reasonable limits and reduce the damage they cause.

Whiteflies are quite common in greenhouses. The safest way to keep the whitefly population under control in a small greenhouse is with the whitefly parasite *Encarsia formosa*, a tiny wasp that is harmless to people or plants. The parasites are available from garden supply catalogs. Release five parasites per square foot of greenhouse area, then keep the temperatures above 70°F so the parasites will thrive. Three releases at two-week intervals will catch the whiteflies at all stages of their life cycle and establish the parasites for the season. Because the parasite population is dependent on the whiteflies as a food source they will not completely eliminate the whiteflies, but they can keep the population low enough to avoid problems. Do not use any pesticides if predators are used or the predators will be killed, too. Using predators outside is not as effective, because they can fly away and eat their fill of whiteflies somewhere else in the neighborhood.

Whiteflies cannot overwinter in cold climate areas but return each year on greenhouse-grown crops or bedding plants brought in from warmer areas. They can also blow in the wind for many miles. Whitefly populations generally peak in August or September then decline.

Aphids are tiny sucking insects that damage the leaves of many plants. They are often tended by ants who feed on the honeydew produced by aphids; ants do not damage leaves. Generally, aphids can be dislodged by spraying with a strong stream of cold water. The spraying must be done daily until aphids are no longer a problem. If there is severe and extensive leaf damage, use chemical control. Many chemical products are labeled for aphids, including Diazinon, malathion, Sevin, and several systemic pesticide formulations. Read the label carefully before purchasing the chemical to make sure your plants are listed on the label. Extremely large trees are best sprayed by a professional as it is difficult to cover the upper leaves with equipment available to the homeowner.

Sow bugs cannot be eliminated using organic methods, but there are ways to protect plants. The sow bug's purpose in life is to help decompose plant material and return it to the soil. Sometimes they also eat fresh plant material, like tender new seedlings. Organic mulch provides all the things a sow bug needs—a dark hiding place, moisture, a source of food. The tricky part is to keep them in the mulch and away from your plants.

To keep the sow bugs under control, avoid overwatering. Mulched areas will need considerably less water than unmulched areas. Water only enough to keep plants from wilting. That amount will depend on the plants, the thickness of the mulch, soil type, and the weather. Also, keep the mulch away from seedlings and tender plants. A small ring of bare soil immediately surrounding the stem of a seedling means the sow bugs will be less likely to find it, especially when they are well fed by the mulch.

Sow bugs can also be trapped by putting small pieces of lumber on the ground then lifting the wood each morning and collecting the sow bugs that are hiding under them. Crush the sow bugs or place them in a container with a small amount of kerosene to kill them.

Thrips are a difficult insect to control on roses and other flowers. They have many generations in a year but are most abundant about the time of the first bloom on roses. They continuously migrate onto the roses from surrounding trees and grass. They then burrow into the bud of the rose, causing distortion and discoloration of the flowers. Thrips can distinguish the color of flowers and seem to prefer yellow and light-colored flowers. A systemic insecticide will protect the flowers for up to ten days. Make sure the plants on which the thrips are feeding are listed on the label of the insecticide. Infested flowers and flower buds should be picked and discarded. The rose will then flower again later in the season when the thrips population is smaller and causes less damage.

Red spider mites are a persistent problem, and few pesticides still on the market will kill them. When they first attack, the best solution is to wash them off the plants with water. They prefer dry, dusty areas and will be discouraged by repeated washing. If washing with water does not combat the spider mites, try pyrethrins or a miticide. Do not use Sevin as it seems to increase spider mite populations.

Insects, like other living things, look for a warm place to spend the winter. Many species go into a dormant state during the winter or burrow into the soil. Others hide under leaves and debris in the yard. Any insects still active in late fall will be looking for a place to hide. They are sometimes attracted to the warmth of the house and come inside. Eliminating their hiding place under leaves and dead plants will reduce the insect population in the garden next year, as the ones without a hiding place will soon freeze.

Of the thousands of beneficial insects, only a few are available commercially. Fortunately beneficial insects are probably already in the yard. Many flies and wasps are beneficial insects; some bugs are; and all lacewings and spiders, although spiders aren't insects. Many of the beneficial insects are small and unnoticeable. Use plants to attract more beneficial insects to the yard. Many of the beneficial insects survive on flower nectar at certain stages of their lives or when insect pests are scarce. Some cultivated flowers produce abundant supplies of nectar and pollen, although wildflowers and herbs seem better for attracting beneficial insects. But many cultivated flowers have been bred for show and have lost some of their nectar-producing qualities. The more diverse the plantings in the yard, the more beneficials they are likely to attract. Start with plants that bloom early in the spring and try to have a constant supply of flowers opening through the summer. If large numbers of pests are congregating on plants, avoid those plants. Even if they provide lots of nectar and pollen, they could attract more pests than beneficial insects.

PARASITES

Dwarf mistletoe does not have leaves like true mistletoe and is entirely parasitic on the tree. It looks like a mass of green twigs growing out of branches on evergreen trees. Over the years it will sap the tree of strength and may kill it. If it is on side branches at some distance from the trunk, prune out those branches. Make the cut in the crotch of a smaller branch or at the trunk. If the mistletoe is on the trunk or on a branch close to the trunk, nothing will kill it without killing the tree.

The visible part is the fruiting part of the plant. The rest of the plant is hidden under the bark of the tree. Anywhere there is swelling, mistletoe is probably growing. The exposed part will produce sticky seeds, shoot them out to land on other evergreens, and start a new mistletoe plant. If other evergreens are in the yard, remove the exposed parts of the mistletoe to keep it from spreading.

Algae can grow in moist, shady areas even in the Southwest. It makes a sort of green slime over the surface of the soil. Although it can be killed by spraying with copper sulfate, it will eventually disappear on its own. If it has never appeared before, it should disappear when the soil dries out and may never come back. Algae can be a recurring problem in areas with poor drainage, heavy shade, and low soil fertility. If it begins to show up every summer, check for soil compaction, then mulch with compost or fertilize the area in the spring.

DISEASES

Powdery mildew is a fungus that makes leaves look as if they have been dusted with flour. Infected leaves usually turn yellow and wither. Severe infections can kill new grass and young plants and may even kill established plants. It occurs mostly in spring or fall when the nights are cool and is more likely to occur in the shade. Severity of the disease can be reduced by applying a fungicide recommended for mildew. Make two applications about ten days apart. If possible, reduce shade the next spring by pruning dense trees and shrubs to prevent reinfection. Most new bluegrass varieties are resistant to powdery mildew, so if necessary overseed or replant with a resistant variety to reduce the problem.

WEEDS

If the soil is tilled to eliminate weeds, many new weed seeds will be brought to the surface and will sprout. Tilling can also spread many perennial weeds and open the site up to erosion. A covering of plants helps prevent the soil from being washed away. If an area is tilled, plant a ground cover and make sure it gets enough moisture to come up. Existing weeds can be used for erosion control, but keep them mowed so the area looks neat. If the weeds are annuals they should be mowed before they go to seed, which will reduce the weed problem. If they are noxious perennial weeds like bindweed or goatheads, they should be removed, including as much of the root as possible, with a hoe or shovel. Native plants will gradually come in and replace the weeds. Mowing a few more times each year could give some of the native grasses an opportunity to get established.

Removing the flowers from dandelions will prevent them from going to seed. This will reduce the number of new dandelions next year, but since dandelions are perennials they should eventually be dug up or killed with herbicide. If herbicides are used, be extremely careful. Herbicides are one of the leading causes of damage to desirable plants in the Southwest. Regular mowing to keep flowers from being produced and digging are the safest means of controlling dandelions in areas where flowers or trees are also present.

Some herbicides will sterilize the ground and prevent any plants from growing for several years. I do not recommend those in urban situations and even hesitate to recommend them for industrial applications. They can kill trees if the roots grow into the sterilized soil; they eventually can wash into nearby areas even though they are tightly bound to soil particles; and bare soil is more easily eroded by wind, causing dust problems. An area where nothing will be grown can be covered with black plastic and mulch. An organic mulch is cooler than rocks or gravel. If trees or shrubs are in the yard, use at least six inches of organic mulch with a woven weed barrier rather than plastic under it. A dense, easy-care ground cover that would outcompete the weeds can also be planted. If the yard is shady, try vinca major or vinca minor. If it is sunny, low-growing junipers, desert zinnia, or wild morning glories might be good choices for hardiness and low water use. Gravel paths and a wood or cement patio can make the backyard a pleasant outdoor room if the soil is covered with drought-tolerant plants.

No chemical pesticides can be used to kill weeds in a flower bed with a variety of plants without killing some of the desirable plants. The best way to remove the weeds is to hoe or pull them. When hoeing, cut the stem of the weed just below the surface of the soil and try not to disturb the soil too much. Many weed seeds need light to germinate; if they are buried deep in the soil, they will never grow. If they are brought to the surface, they will sprout.

CHAPTER 11

Houseplants

GENERAL CARE

Some plants like bright, direct sunlight all day; others don't ever want the sun shining directly on their leaves. Light requirements of many houseplants are listed at the end of this chapter. The majority of houseplants should be watered when the top inch or so of soil is dry. Test this by feeling the soil. One of the biggest problems beginners have with houseplants is overwatering them. The results of overwatering can actually look the same as underwatering. When the roots and stems rot, the water cannot get to the leaves, so they dry up.

To water by a schedule, soak the soil once a week. Add water until it begins to drain out the bottom of the pot, then don't touch it for another week. Always pot plants in a container with holes in the bottom. This container should then be put in another container or saucer without holes to protect the furniture or carpet. Plants in plastic pots require less frequent watering than those in clay pots because plastic prevents water from evaporating. If the soil stays damp most of the time, root rot and stem rot are likely to occur.

Plants will stay healthy for up to two weeks during a vacation if the heat is turned down so the temperature stays between 55 and 60°F. Water the plants before leaving, making sure the rootball is entirely moist. Group the plants together in an area where they will not be in direct sunlight but will get bright light. Put a loose plastic tent over the plants. A dry cleaning bag draped over the plants will work well.

It is normal for houseplants to lose leaves when they get less light. Since sunlight is reduced in winter, plants often lose some leaves at that time. Hanging plants look particularly straggly when this happens. If there is healthy growth in the center of the pot, prune back all the hanging stems. Cut them back to a bud at the edge of the pot and they should put out new growth as the days begin to get longer. By summer the plant will look as good as new. Other houseplants will branch out more naturally as the light increases in the spring. Certain stresses, such as moving the plant, a change in temperature, or a change in watering practices, can cause the weeping fig to drop many of its leaves. The leaves of the weeping fig, and most other houseplants, do not last forever. Every year a few of them will fall off. Do not try to correct the problem on plants like weeping fig except by supplemental light.

Plants have the ability to clean the air both by trapping particulate matter like dust and by absorbing pollutants. As a general rule low-light plants seem to be best at removing pollutants from the air. Philodendrons and philodendron-like plants, Chinese evergreens, dracaenas, spider plants, ivies, and spathiphyllums are among the best pollution collectors. NASA research has shown that these plants remove benzene, formaldehyde, carbon monoxide, and other trace pollutants from the air. About fifteen to twenty plants will help purify the air in an eighteen-hundred-square-foot house.

Almost any houseplant can be put outside for the summer given the right conditions. Very few houseplants can tolerate full sun outdoors. Some require partial shade; others prefer full shade. Put the houseplants that prefer low light levels under heavy shade like a mulberry tree or on a north-facing, covered balcony or patio. Other houseplants can go under lighter shade or be protected by shadecloth for the summer. Water the plants more frequently when they are outside exposed to the heat and wind. Check them at least twice a week to be sure they are not too dry.

Houseplants that have spent the summer outdoors should be brought in before the nighttime temperatures reach 40°F. They may be damaged by temperatures that are above freezing but too cold for most tropical houseplants. Night temperatures drop in early fall, so to be on the safe side bring tender houseplants inside in August. Geraniums, sansevieria, and other somewhat hardier plants can stay outside for a few weeks longer.

Before bringing any plants indoors, clean the pot and the plant with plain water; inspect plants carefully for insects or diseases. If necessary, spray the plant with an insecticide or fungicide before bringing it into the house. If the plant has become severely diseased during the summer, it may be better to discard the plant and purchase a new plant for the house.

A number of houseplants are particularly easy to grow. Asparagus fern, Chinese evergreen, rubber plant, philodendron, jade plant, geranium, and spider plants are all easy-to-care-for plants. They tolerate a variety of conditions. For the look of ferns in a house that is not humid enough to keep them alive, try an asparagus fern. Three types are available, and all of them prefer an east window or filtered light rather than a south or west window. A Chinese evergreen can take very dim light and warm temperatures, making them excellent apartment plants. Put them in a corner that gets a little light and water them when they really dry out. Rubber plants and philodendrons also tolerate low-light conditions. Both should dry out between watering, and neither likes dust on its leaves, but other than that they aren't particular. Jade plants and geraniums do well inside with sun, heat, and dry soil. Both can be put outside in the summer and brought back in when freezing temperatures approach, although the geraniums should be replaced if they get leggy. The jade plant will get bigger and bigger year after year. The spider plant is among the easiest houseplants to grow. It can take either sun or filtered light, has fleshy roots that keep the plant alive for some time if it isn't watered, and will produce plenty of offspring if it gets potbound.

Many miniature plants do well in terrariums, and some stores even have sections devoted to terrarium plants. Small African violets, baby's tears, artillery plants, aluminum plants, creeping figs, coleus, small Chinese evergreens, English ivy, fittonias, little ferns, miniature sansevieria, small aralias, mosses, peperomias, and small, slow-growing palms do well in terrariums. Do not select too many plants for a terrarium. To get an idea of what they will look like, arrange them on the countertop before putting them in the container.

Take the time to give the plant roots a healthy environment before you plant. Start with a thin layer of charcoal on the bottom of the container. Cover this with about half an inch of gravel, then add an inch or more of potting soil. Make sure the soil is evenly moist but not soggy before planting.

The trick to keeping a terrarium looking nice is to make sure it gets enough light, but no direct sunlight. Pinch the plants back as they start to outgrow the container. Some plants such as aralias, palms, and African violets should not be pinched back. Be sure to get slow-growing or miniature forms of these plants. Terrariums only need water occasionally. Add a little water when the soil appears dry.

The part of the root that absorbs water and nutrients is the root hairs. Root hairs are only found within millimeters of the root tip and live for only about three days. They are very tender and can easily be injured in the transplanting process. A number of environmental factors affect the number of root hairs, the foremost being the availability of water and oxygen.

To avoid damaging the tender root hairs, do not let the roots dry out when plants are transplanted. To assure success, dampen the potting soil slightly before potting. It should feel moist but still be rather crumbly. To pot uprooted cuttings, put some potting soil in the bottom of the pot, remove the plant from the water, and hold it at the correct planting level as soil is carefully placed around the roots. Press lightly on the soil when the roots are covered. Do not pack the soil into the pot as this could damage the roots. Water the plant immediately until water runs out the bottom of the pot. Do not fertilize the plant until the roots have had a chance to become well established in the soil. Using this procedure, new plants should survive the transplanting process with a minimum of shock.

If a plant is getting too large for the space it is in, remove the plant from the pot and slice off some of the roots. Remove some of the surface soil, clean the pot, and put the plant back in with new potting soil. This is essentially a bonsai technique, used to keep plants from growing too large for confined spaces. The top of the plant will probably need pruning after the roots are pruned. This technique is best used on plants with several growing points, like many philodendrons, weeping fig, and vigorously growing ferns.

To keep plants from growing too quickly, avoid fertilizing them except when they show signs of fertilizer deficiency. If the leaves are pale, yellow, or purplish and they are not supposed to be, fertilize the plant. Otherwise simply water it when necessary and keep it in an area with adequate light.

Houseplants with smooth leaves should be cleaned with plain water. Do not use detergent, which can be toxic to some plants. Milk and many of the products that are sold to make leaves shinier contain oils that clog the pores on the leaves, so it is generally not advisable to use those. Plain water will get the dust off, and the natural waxes in healthy leaves will provide enough shine to make the plants look good. The simplest way to clean the plants is to wash them in the shower. Adjust the water so that it is just a little cooler than room temperature. Plants can be injured by hot water, but many houseplants are tropical plants and cannot stand extremely cold tap water. Rub the leaves lightly with a cloth to remove all the dust. The shower will also leach excess salts and minerals out of the soil.

If the plant is too big to move to the shower, wipe the dust off the leaves with a damp cloth. If the leaves have a heavy buildup of dust, change the water frequently so that little mud spots are not left behind on the leaves.

Hairy-leafed plants may collect even more dust than smooth-leafed plants. However, they generally cannot tolerate water on their leaves or dusting with a cloth. Blow the dust off of small plants like African violets. Larger hairy-leafed houseplants with a lot of dust on them can be very carefully vacuumed with a small, handheld vacuum. Take care not to injure the leaves, and do not try this with a carpet vacuum.

Most foliage houseplants, which are generally tropical plants, tend to go dormant during the winter. Low levels of light do not allow them to produce enough food, so they may drop the least productive leaves in order to make sure the entire plant survives. Avoid overwatering or fertilizing them at this time. Water and fertilizer will make them more susceptible to disease. By February they should be growing again and put on new leaves. When signs of new growth appear, fertilize them with a dilute, water soluble fertilizer. Continue fertilizing them once a month until November and they should have enough food reserves to last through the winter.

Winter-flowering plants generally thrive in cooler temperatures. Plants such as cyclamen, Christmas and Easter cactus, and poinsettia need plenty of water and fertilizer in the winter to produce their flowers.

INSECTS

Fungus gnats do not eat plants or bite people, but they can be irritating when large numbers of them are flying around in the house. Their larvae live on organic matter in potting soil. Adults do not feed on plant material and don't live very long. Conditions that favor the development of fungi, such as excessive soil moisture, contribute to increases in fungus gnats. Houseplants are often overwatered during the winter. The plant uses less water so the soil stays moist longer. The most effective means of controlling fungus gnats is to reduce the frequency of watering.

Not many effective chemical controls are available. Because the lar vae are in the soil, a soil drench is the most effective means of control. An experimental method using a dilute soap or detergent drench has been used successfully in some cases, but this can injure the plant if not done properly. Pyrethroid houseplant insecticides can kill some adults. Repeated applications of houseplant insecticides every two to three days may help reduce populations, but nothing will be effective unless efforts are also made to limit soil moisture.

OTHER PROBLEMS

Several fungi can cause plants to rot off. They are present in all soils, and spores are floating around in the air. To avoid or completely kill off the fungi is impossible, but it is possible to make it more difficult for them to grow. When temperatures are cooler and plants are not growing very fast, they use less water. Let the soil dry out between waterings.

Mineral buildup on the surface of the soil can also damage the stems of plants, allowing fungi to enter. If there is a white, yellowish, or brown crust on the surface of the potting soil or around the edges of the pot, scrape off the top inch or so of soil and leach the remaining soil by filling the pots with water several times and letting the water drain out completely. Then put fresh potting soil in to replace what was taken out. Over-fertilization can cause mineral buildup on the soil and fungal growth.

Frequently the salts in the water build up and make the soil somewhat water resistant. When the soil dries out completely it will no longer absorb water. The plant may also be rootbound, which causes it to dry out quickly. To leach excess salts out of the soil, the water must penetrate the soil. Put the plants in the sink or bathtub without saucers or containers under them. Fill the pot with water then make holes in the soil surface with a probe like a screwdriver or knife. As the water drains down these holes, check to see if the soil is absorbing it by pushing your finger into the soil close to the hole. If the subsurface soil is absorbing water, keep watering and making holes until the soil is saturated. If not, make a solution of about one gallon of water and two or three drops of dishwashing liquid. Water the plant with that a little at a time until the soil begins absorbing water. Once the soil in the pot is completely wet, water a few more times to remove the soap and the remaining salt. If the soil is packed tightly with roots, allow the pot to drain overnight then repot the plant. Before placing the plant in the larger pot, loosen the roots at the side of the rootball so they will be able to grow into the new soil.

Overfertilization will cause the leaf tips of many plants, especially spider plants, to turn brown. Chlorine or hard water will cause the same problem. Spider plants without brown-tipped leaves are unusual. If the brown extends up into the leaf more than about half an inch, try to leach out the fertilizer and minerals. Water the plant until the water comes out the holes in the bottom. Let it drain, then fill the pot with water again. Repeat this procedure three times. That should remove enough of the excess fertilizer or minerals to allow the plant to begin to regain its health. Watering with distilled water can prevent this problem.

After all this washing and watering, let the surface of the soil dry out thoroughly before watering again. The plant will start to rot in the center if it is watered too frequently. If it starts to rot, it is likely to die.

PROPAGATION

Most houseplants can be propagated either by cutting off a section of stem and putting it in water or soil to form roots or by dividing a plant with more than one growing point. It is difficult to get cuttings of a large-leafed plant, such as ficus or rubber tree, to root under normal household conditions because most houses are too dry. The leaves of such plants are so large they lose too much water before the roots form. They can be propagated by air layering. This technique allows the roots of the established plant to continue feeding the leaves of the new plant as new roots are established. Get some rooting hormone, which is available in most garden supply centers, a small amount of long-fibered sphagnum moss, string, plastic wrap, and foil. Soak a couple of handfuls of the moss in water until it is completely saturated. About three inches below the lowest leaf, make a slanting cut in the stem of the plant. Do not cut through more than half of the stem. Hold the cut open with a toothpick or matchstick and dab some rooting hormone on the exposed surfaces. Stuff some of the moss into the cut, being careful not to break the remaining stem, and wrap a baseball-size mass of the moist sphagnum moss around the entire stem where the cut was made. Cover the sphagnum moss with plastic wrap to keep the moisture in. Tie both ends of the plastic wrap. Cover the entire ball with foil. This will make it dark inside the sphagnum ball and encourage roots to come to the surface where they can be seen. Check the sphagnum every few weeks to make sure it is still moist. When roots have filled the entire sphagnum ball, which can take several days to a few months, cut off the new plant just below the sphagnum ball and plant it in a pot. It will need to be misted or placed in a pebble tray full of water for the first few weeks until it is well established. If several branches of the large rubber tree or ficus are air layered, the original plant will have a unique shape, which may or may not be attractive. You may want to dicard the old plant when new ones are well established.

To propagate dieffenbachia, cut off the entire plant and cut the cane into pieces, each of which contains at least one node (the lines around the stem where the leaves were attached). Lay the stem pieces on their side in a large pot filled with potting soil. The stem should be about half buried in the soil. In a few weeks, roots will grow from the stem into the soil, then leaves will sprout. Each section of cane can produce a new plant. The roots and small portion of stem in the original pot will probably sprout leaves, too.

Normally, dieffenbachia canes sprout within a few weeks, but not always. If the cuttings were from a woody part of the stem or taken when the plant was approaching dormancy, it could take several months. Keep watering them and don't throw them away unless they rot.

AFRICAN VIOLETS

Despite their reputation, African violets are relatively easy to take care of. They need to be planted in an organic potting soil. Commercial African violet potting soils are available in stores. Place the plant where it will get bright light but no direct sunlight. It may help to place a tray of pebbles under the plant, and keep the tray filled with water to the top of the pebbles. Turn the plant often to make it grow symmetrically, and leave it in the same pot until it is completely potbound. It will bloom better if it is a little crowded.

The most common problem with African violets is overwatering. Feel the soil before watering and water only if it is dry just below the surface. Always water your African violets with water that is room temperature. Water either from the top or the bottom, but be consistent. To water from the top, pour water carefully around the plant. Do not get water on the leaves. To water from the bottom, a wick system is the best choice. Special pots are available for wick watering, or you can make one by threading a piece of soft cotton cord through the hole in the bottom on the pot. Pull the cord up into the soil as the African violet is planted in the pot. Leave four to six inches sticking out the bottom. Elevate the pot slightly so that it does not sit on the wick. Place the pot in a saucer and put water in the saucer until it just reaches the bottom of the pot. A simpler way to water from the bottom is to put the pot in a generous saucer and fill the saucer with water. A few hours later come back and pour off the excess water. Remember to pour off the water or the roots may rot and the African violet will die.

If the water is salty, watering African violets from above is preferable to wick watering. Give the plant a little extra water each time, then empty the dish under the pot. This leaches out some of the salt in the soil. With wick watering, the salt continues to build up in the soil as the water evaporates. This can injure the plants. For those who have trouble remembering to water the African violets before they are completely dried out, wick watering is an appropriate solution, but water them with distilled water with a very, very dilute fertilizer solution added. African violets should be fertilized regularly with a balanced, water soluble fertilizer. A balanced fertilizer is one that does not have any o's in the analysis.

Several pests bother African violets. For an inexperienced grower, throwing the plant away if problems develop and buying a new one is the best solution. If a favorite variety develops a problem, start a new plant. Cut off a leaf with one-half to one inch of the petiole (leaf stem) and stick it in a peat moss–perlite mixture up to the leaf. Several small plantlets will grow from the base of one leaf. When the plants have at least two leaves that are more than one-quarter of an inch across, it is time to separate and plant them. Carefully remove the whole clump from the soil and gently pull the little plants apart. Plant each one that has at least one good root attached. Some of the plants will not survive, but some will, and they will be better shaped as they mature if they are separated rather then planting them as a clump. They will be ready to pot in about three months but will require several more months to flower.

Most aspects of growing miniature African violets are the same as growing the larger varieties. The biggest difference is that the pots in which the miniatures are grown are so small that the potting soil cannot hold much water. They will not flower well in pots that are too large, so they need special attention to watering. Most miniature African violets come with special pots with little wicks. The wicks go into a reservoir of water and keep the potting soil from drying out. If it is not in one of those special pots, put the miniature African violet in a small pot and remember to water it frequently. Daily watering may be necessary.

AVOCADOS

Avocados prefer humid coastal areas without the extremes we have here, so it is difficult to keep them healthy for long periods of time. Putting the pot on pebbles in a tray with water up to the top of the pebbles will help increase the humidity surrounding the plants and could keep the leaves from drying up and falling off.

If the soil in the pot is heavy, it will hold water, thus requiring less frequent watering. Water the plant until water comes out the bottom of the pot, then don't water it again until the first inch of soil feels dry. If there are no holes in the pot, make some holes so excess water can drain out.

As avocado trees grow and mature, the stem will turn brown as it starts to get bark. The natural growth pattern for avocados is to grow straight up for several feet before putting out side branches. As they grow, the leaves will fall off the bottom half of the tree. To encourage side growth, pinch out the tip growth. If the leaves are falling off the top half of the tree, it could be either a salt problem or lack of water. If the light is too intense, the water could be evaporating from the leaves faster than the roots can pick it up. This is not a problem in a house but in a greenhouse a young avocado tree should be partially shaded, especially in summer.

Salt can accumulate in the soil either from water or from fertilizers. If the leaves have brown edges, do not fertilize the trees for a while. If they seem to have stopped growing, fertilize again.

AMARYLLIS

The production of large numbers of leaves means an amaryllis bulb will be able to store energy to produce flowers next year. One of the best ways to get a bulb to produce lots of leaves is to put it outside in the summer. Do not leave it outside too long because amaryllis bulbs are sensitive to frost. Dig it up as soon as the leaves start to die back. If the leaves do not begin to turn yellow by late September dig up the bulb and bring it inside with the leaves still on it. Remove most of the soil and all the dried leaves from the bulb. Plant it in well-drained potting soil in a pot just slightly larger than the bulb. Put the bulb in a cool, dark place until new growth starts, then place it in a bright place out of direct sunlight. Be careful not to overwater the bulb while it has no leaves or flower stalk.

CYCLAMEN

One variety of cyclamen is hardy outside, but the variety sold in garden centers and flower shops as a gift plant is not. It cannot survive freezing temperatures. Cyclamen are cool-season plants, and they have corms, which are similar to bulbs, that lie dormant during the summer. After a cyclamen has finished flowering, the leaves will start to die back. At the base of the plant is the corm. Cut the dry leaves off without damaging the corm and put the pot in a cool place. A north-facing window sill is a good location. Do not fertilize it while it is resting; water it only occasionally. When it sprouts leaves later in the summer, start watering it more frequently. Fertilize it with dilute, water soluble fertilizer at that time.

FERNS

Although most people consider ferns delicate, a Boston fern can take quite a bit of abuse. They are easily divided. Get some potting soil and a couple of extra pots. Moisten the potting soil and mix the water in well before starting. The procedure is rather messy and is best done outside. Take the fern out to the work area and examine the bottom of the pot. If there are large sprouts growing out of the bottom, break them off, with as much crown and root as possible, and pot them in another pot. Discard any sprouts that break off without bringing with them a large section of crown tissue. Look among the fronds for the crown of the plant. The plant will probably have several growing points. Each of these can be divided into a separate plant, although it will take a long time for the plant to refill the pot. Knock the plant out of the pot and tear the root ball in half or quarters. Select the most attractively shaped section and center it in the original pot. Fill in around the roots with potting soil, water it well, then add more potting soil if necessary. Be sure to leave about an inch or so at the top of the pot so water will not spill over the edge. Put the other sections in other pots. They make excellent gifts for birthdays, housewarmings, retirement parties, or other special occasions.

Although most ferns do not need direct sunlight, they do need bright filtered light. For the ferns to do well there should be enough light to cast a shadow. If they do not receive this much light, either move the ferns or buy some lights. For ferns, florescent lights are best but incandescent lights will work. Keep the lights on twelve hours per day. Ferns also do better when the humidity is high. Keep them in a bathroom, where humidity is generally higher or place them on a tray of gravel, filling the tray with water almost to the top of the gravel.

Ferns, bromeliads, and many other houseplants need filtered sunlight if they are placed outside. They can be kept on the north side of the house or under a group of trees where they will be shaded all day long during the summer. Constructing a shade house is another possibility. A lathhouse is the most attractive structure. A frame covered with shadecloth will also give the plants the protection they need. To build the structure use two-by-four framing on four-foot centers. The frame can be covered with shadecloth or with three-quarter-inch lath spaced one inch apart.

Be sure to watch the plants carefully and control any insects or diseases immediately. Inspect the plants and the pots for evidence of insects or disease before taking them inside in the fall.

GERANIUMS

Geraniums can be stored by digging them up and hanging them upside down in a cool place. The temperature in the storage area should be an even 50°F. This is a problem in most of the Southwest because garages and sheds tend to get too hot and dehydrate plants and roots during the day or get too cold and freeze them at night. Try putting a few in pots and keep them as houseplants in case some stored ones freeze or become dehydrated over the course of the winter.

If you have enough room for several houseplants, dig up one of each variety and let the others freeze rather than trying to store them. In the spring, break off the branches of the houseplants and start new plants from these. Rooting geraniums is rather simple but a few tricks will make success more likely. Start by selecting the branches of the parent plant for cuttings. Grasp the upper stem firmly and break off the end of the branch. It will break at the point where it is still soft enough to make new roots but is mature, or hard enough to avoid rotting. Next, remove all flowers or flower buds from the cuttings. They will need to put their energy into forming new roots, not into flowering. Let the cuttings sit on the counter overnight. This begins the process of forming callus, the tissue from which new root growth will start. If the callus is formed before the cutting is put in soil, disease organisms will be blocked from entering the stem and the plant is not likely to rot. After the plants have sat for at least ten to twelve hours, stick the stem about an inch to an inch and a half into moist potting soil. Water to eliminate air pockets around the stem and put the cuttings in a brightly lit area but not in direct sunlight. New roots should be formed in a few weeks. Repot the cuttings, plant them outside if the weather is warm enough, or move them to a permanent location indoors.

Scented and ivy-leafed geraniums are *Pelargoniums* as are common geraniums. Plants with the scientific name *Geranium* are the wildflowers called cranesbill. Scented geraniums are a different species from the common or garden geranium. The ivy-leafed geranium is *Pelargonium peltatum*. It has glossy, bright green, ivylike leaves and trailing stems that can be two to three feet long. The flowers can be either single or double.

Scented geraniums can be used in sachets or potpourri or for flavoring jellies or scenting finger bowls. Most people simply enjoy the smell when they brush against the foliage. Geraniums may smell like lemon, lime, roses, apples, or peppermint. Each of these is a different species of *Pelargonium*.

Tobacco budworms can be a problem on geraniums. The tiny rust-color or green-striped caterpillars grow up to be moths with light green wings with four oblique light bands on them. The wingspan of the moths is one and a half inches. Eggs are laid singly on the underside of the leaves, and the larvae pupate in the soil. There are generally two generations of the budworms per year. When they are present, they can be controlled with *Bacillus thuringiensis* (BT) or Sevin.

ORCHIDS

Orchids are found in all sorts of climates, but many of the popular varieties come from tropical forests. Even in tropical forests temperature and humidity vary depending on altitude and latitude. Many orchids do well with night temperatures of 55 to 65°F and day temperatures of 62 to 80°F. They do best when the humidity is above 30 percent. Fortunately, these conditions are very comfortable for people too, so a number of orchids do well as houseplants.

Orchid varieties sold as houseplants are generally either terrestrial or epiphytic. Terrestrial orchids are plants that grow from bulbs, much like lilies or hyacinths. The epiphytic group grows on rocks and trees, off the forest floor. They derive their nutrients from the air and from decaying material that falls into the same crevice as the orchid seed. The terrestrial ones grow in organic potting soil; the epiphytic ones grow on moist sphagnum moss or shredded bark.

Buy orchids from a nursery where advice from experienced orchid growers is available, and make sure the varieties will do well as houseplants. A number of good books are available on orchid culture. Garden clubs devoted to growing orchids can also provide advice for novice orchid growers.

PLANTS FOR LOW-LIGHT CONDITIONS

	WATER	TEMPERATURE
Cast iron plant	Average	Cool
Chinese evergreen	Average	Warm
Fittonia	Average	Warm
Maidenhair fern	Moist	Average
Parlor palm	Average	Warm
Sansevieria[a]	Average to Dry	Warm

[a] Sansevieria appears in each table because it is a highly tolerant and adaptable plant.

PLANTS FOR MEDIUM-LIGHT CONDITIONS

	WATER	TEMPERATURE
Aucuba	Average	Cool
Asparagus fern	Average	Average
Begonia	Average	Average
Boston fern	Average	Cool
Norfolk island pine	Average	Cool
Peperomia	Average	Warm
Philodendron	Average	Warm
Sansevieria	Average to Dry	Warm
Staghorn fern	Average	Cool
Swedish ivy	Average	Average
Weeping fig	Average	Warm

PLANTS FOR BRIGHT-LIGHT CONDITIONS

	WATER	TEMPERATURE
Agave	Dry	Cool
Aloe	Dry	Cool
Croton	Average	Warm
Crown of thorns	Dry	Average
Dieffenbachia	Average	Warm
Dracena	Average	Warm
Jade plant	Dry	Cool
Kalanchoe	Average	Cool
Sansevieria	Average to Dry	Warm
Scheflera	Average	Warm

INDEX

120; peaches, 60, 111,
113, 120, 121
fungi, 7, 44, 71, 78, 89, 90,
125, 182, 197, 212, 213
fungicide, 44, 89, 90, 204,
209
fungus gnats, 212
fusarium, 44, 179

gaillardia, 143, 146
gall, 89
garden designer, 22
gayfeather, 126, 146–49
geraniums, 125, 133, 134,
141, 209, 220–22
globe amaranth, 130, 149
gloxinia, 149
glyphosate, 47, 48, 107, 173,
189, 195, 196
golden current, 100
goldenrod, 145, 149
grape hyacinth, 135, 145
grapes, 89,119,120
grapevines, 24, 119
grass, 2, 6–11, 13, 15, 16,
26–29, 31, 32, 35–45,
47–49, 81, 82, 113, 145,
164, 202, 204
grass clippings, 6–8, 11, 13,
38, 40, 164
greenhouse, 141, 142, 152,
180, 194–96, 198, 201, 218
gypsum, 5

hedge, 98, 99, 102, 132, 133,
156
herbicide, 37, 47, 48, 80, 86,
107, 191, 196, 205

herbs, 146, 150, 157, 168,
184, 186, 195, 203
holly, 25, 102
hollyhock, 125, 126
honeylocus, 9, 102
horse, 5
horseradish, 173
hosta, 145
houseplants,145, 207–09,
211, 212, 214, 220–22
hummingbirds, 25
humus, 6

impatiens, 125, 133, 142,
144, 145, 195
Indian ricegrass, 49, 148
insecticide, 84, 87, 88, 118,
183, 192, 193, 195, 200,
202, 209
IPM, 85, 87
iris, 127, 140, 141, 146
iron, 4, 42, 66–68, 223
irrigation: bubblers, 31–32;
drip, 30–32; efficiency, 19;
flowers, 31, 148; fruit, 109,
112; groundcovers, 31, 48;
houseplants, 207, 210,
216–17,223; lawns,
27–30, 32–33, 36, 38–39;
roses, 151–52; salty soil, 4;
sprinkler, 27–30; summer,
32–33, vegetables, 31,
160, 166, 169, 182; win-
ter, 31 ivy, 97, 107, 145,
149, 150, 199, 210, 221,
223

jade plant, 209, 223

juniper,16, 53, 93, 102

kerria japonica, 144
kohlrabi, 165

landscape architects, 14, 21,
22
landscape contractors, 21, 22
landscape plan, 17
larkspur, 149
last frost date, 127, 128, 158,
162, 163
lavender cotton, 97
lawn clippings, 40
lawnmowers, 82, 85
lawns,6, 10, 16, 19, 20, 27,
28, 32, 35–40, 42, 44–46,
48, 81, 82, 130, 196
leaching, 10, 29
leaf mold,8, 9
lettuce, 23, 129, 158, 159,
161, 165, 168, 179
lilac,86, 87, 102, 103, 143,
149
lily,141, 144, 149, 192
lily of the valley,144, 149
linden, 81
lisianthus,143;
loam, 1, 31, 43, 160
longhorn beetle, 86
low voltage lights, 23

magnolia, 58, 97; mahonia,
25, 97, 102, 144; maiden
grass, 49;
manure, 5, 6, 10–13, 39, 62,
103, 124, 136, 146, 160,
170, 176, 177